T. W. WEST

Discovering
Scottish
Architecture

SHIRE PUBLICATIONS LTD

Contents

ACKNOWLEDGEMENTS

Photographs are acknowledged as follows: Cadbury Lamb, plates 1, 3, 5, 6, 9, 11, 12, 15, 16, 19, 20, 23, 25, 26, 31, 32, 36, 37, 38, 39, 40, 42, 45, 46, 47, 48, 49, 51, 52, 53; the Scottish Tourist Board, plates 17, 28; Geoffrey N. Wright, plates 2, 4, 7, 8, 10, 13, 14, 18, 21, 22, 24, 27, 29, 30, 33, 34, 35, 41, 43, 44, 50.
The cover photograph, by Cadbury Lamb, is of Drumlanrig Castle, Dumfries and Galloway.

Set in 9 point Times roman and printed in Great Britain by C. I. Thomas & Sons (Haverfordwest) Ltd, Press Buildings, Merlins Bridge, Haverfordwest, Dyfed.

1. Prehistoric, Roman and Celtic

The prehistoric period

The earliest man-made structures to survive from the neolithic period in Scotland are the so-called chambered cairns or family tombs of the earliest farming communities. These ossuaries date from 2000 BC and are elongated dry-stone structures built mainly of medium-sized stones. They are often corbelled right over with overlapping stones or roofed with large lintel stones. Entered by a portal, the burial chamber is sometimes reached by a passage. The chamber or gallery is compartmented and the whole structure covered by a shaped mound of earth or stones, rounded or elongated, that may be as much as 100 feet (30 m) long.

There are several types of chambered cairn. One is 'horned', with a pair of curved lines of upright stones branching out from one end and enclosing a semicircular space.

Maes Howe in Stenness (Orkney) is round with a passage 100 feet (30 m) in diameter and encircled by a large ditch. Its beautifully masoned corbelled chamber gives access to three tiny burial cells, and on its walls it records in runes the visits of Orcadian crusaders in the twelfth century. Presumably the grave of a chief, it is one of the grandest chambered cairns in western Europe and a fine achievement of an early technology.

At Camster, just north of Lybster (Highland), are two megalithic chambered tombs, the Grey Cairns. One is a 'horned' two-chambered elongated cairn; the other is round and contains a single chamber reached by a passage.

At Skara Brae in the Orkneys, 7 miles (11 km) south of Stromness, is one of the most remarkable prehistoric sites in Britain, a neolithic village — rather later than 2000 BC — containing the earliest dwellings to have survived, under a cover of sand dunes. This was a small community of stock farmers, who also collected shellfish and lived in rectangular dry-stone huts, about 20 by 15 feet (6.1 by 4.6 m), with rounded corners. In the middle of each hut was a kerbed hearth and on either side were box bunks, partitioned off by stone slabs. Above these were recessed squares or 'cupboards', and there were slabbed tanks in the floor and a 'dresser' of two shelves. Cells in the walls of these houses may have been 'pantries' or privies, since some have drains running into a main sewer. A stone slab, secured by a bar, closed the low doorway. The roofs have not survived but above and around the houses was heaped midden material mixed with sand and held by retaining walls. As the midden accumulated the passageways between the eight separate huts were faced and roofed in to become stone connecting tunnels.

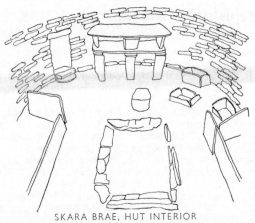

SKARA BRAE, HUT INTERIOR

No more than foundation traces — the familiar 'hut circles' of the moors — which once had low turf walls and a pointed roof of turf supported by a centre pole and radiating 'rafters' — remain of most bronze age dwellings.

Cairns and earthen barrows of this period are invariably round, usually containing only small cists made of stone slabs. There are many henges or ritual stone circles, some surrounding burial cairns. Those with a concentric ditch round the ring of standing stones or monoliths are known as 'fossed' circles.

Among the most outstanding works of this period are the fine bronze age stone burial cairn of Memsie near Fraserburgh (Grampian), the cairns and stone circle in Strathclyde between Nether Largie and Kilmartin, on an important routeway (with which may be seen a megalithic chambered cairn of earlier neolithic date), and the site at Cairnpapple Hill by Torphichen (Lothian), where a neolithic sanctuary became a bronze age fossed circle.

Other remarkable stone circles include the splendid fossed circle known as the Ring of Brodgar (Orkney), Auchagallon

CRANNOG

circle (Arran, Strathclyde), the 'recumbent' stone circle — representative of a type from the north-east — at Loanhead, near Daviot (Grampian), and above all the Standing Stones at Callanish (Lewis, Western Isles), a whole complex of megaliths based on a circle with a long and short avenue on opposite sides and two short arms projecting at right angles to complete the cross effect. It was probably not conceived as a whole, however, but extended over a long period.

A rare and outstanding site is the late bronze age village at Jarlshof near Sumburgh (Shetland) consisting of a number of oval, stone-built dwellings all surrounded by a dry-stone wall. Each house is like a miniature courtyard, where five corbelled cells are grouped round a central hearth, probably an open one. The cell opposite the doorway is larger and may have been a stall for animals. Here there are also late iron age houses of the 'Pictish wheel' type with parts of their roofs intact — large, round, stone-walled buildings divided into segmental compartments (leaving a large central space) by radially placed slabs, which served as roof supports where there was no timber available for the more usual concentric rings of upright posts. The latest period of settlement belonged to the Viking period from the ninth to the thirteenth centuries and these are the remains of one of the most complete Norse villages — with characteristic long houses — in the British Isles.

The settled plough cultivation and animal husbandry of the Celts was conducted from so-called 'hillforts' or fortified hilltop villages, necessary owing to inter-tribal strife. These consisted of a large irregular area, in which were grouped round dwellings, surrounded by massive defensive ramparts of palisaded earth or dry-stone wall with a ditch and counterscarp and another palisaded earth rampart and ditch. Causeways and gateways gave access to the central area. Near Brechin (Tayside) are the White and Brown Caterthuns, the first of which has four ramparts and ditches arranged concentrically and crossed by entrance causeways. Sometimes the walling was bonded together by vertical beams of timber which, when set on fire, fused the rubble. Traprain Law (Lothian) is an example of these 'vitrified' or 'Gallic' forts.

Romano-British 'crannogs', or lake dwellings erected on piles or made of earth and stones, were exceptionally long-lived and sites include Milton Loch (Dumfries and Galloway) and Lochlie, near Tarbolton (Strathclyde).

The Romano-British earth houses or 'weems', found only in the east, are underground stone structures consisting of galleries, large trenches or chambers, up to 80 feet (24 m) in length and lined with stone. Occasionally they have an inner chamber opening off with a 'beehive' roof, that is corbelled in towards the

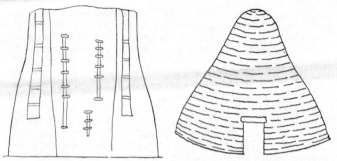

BROCH OF MOUSA   BEEHIVE HUT

centre like a bee skep. The sides of the gallery are also corbelled in until close enough to be spanned by roof lintels. These are now thought of as refuges, not dwellings, and probably some were in use centuries later at the time of the Viking raids — at Ardestie and Carlungie near Dundee (Tayside) are the remains of round huts that constituted the farm above ground.

At Culsh near Tarland (Grampian), the roofing slabs are preserved over a large chamber and entrance, whilst other examples with stairs, passages and roofs supported by stone pillars may be seen in the vicinity of Kirkwall (Orkney). There is an interesting small iron age fort with an earth house in its rock-cut ditch at Glencorse (Lothian).

There are remains of over four hundred brochs of the first to the fifth centuries. Seemingly the work of settlers from south-west Britain, they are usually found on the coasts and straths of the north-west and north. The highest of these roughly resembled a miniature modern cooling tower in form, though the batter of the outside gives a different profile. The famous Broch of Mousa (Shetland) is 43 feet (13 m) high whilst the largest, Edin's Hall (one of the few to be found in the Lowlands), on the side of Cockburn Law (Borders), is 55 feet (17 m) in diameter.

The ground floor commonly consisted of a solid circular dry-stone wall 10 to 20 feet (3-6 m) thick enclosing a court of 20 to 30 feet (6-9 m) across. A tunnel closed by a stone slab led through the wall, which also contained a small number of intramural corbelled cells; one on the left of the entrance, a storehouse cell, had a clockwise stair leading through about half the circumference to a parapet and another controlled the door bar. Round the central living space ran a penthouse type verandah (or it may have been roofed over). In the middle was a rectangular hearth and nearby a well chamber or cistern.

It was frequently the practice to construct, rising above the massive ground-floor wall, two concentric walls, one vertical, the other one battered to produce the characteristic profile. These walls were bonded by horizontal slabs forming pavements for the galleries, which were interrupted by the stair rising within the hollow of the wall. Though there were no openings in the outer wall, four slits ran up the inner wall. A notable feature of brochs is the quality of their neat, well dressed masonry. But as they were occupied for several centuries they underwent remodelling. Most are surrounded by a defensive wall, within which are hut remains. Edin's Hall was defended by a series of outworks. Other brochs are near Brora, Glenelg (both Highland), Dun Carloway (Lewis, Western Isles) and Gurness (Orkney). In the Hebrides are many small stone-walled forts known as 'duns', also occupied over a very long period. They are not more than two storeys high but enclose larger and less regular areas: some have galleries. They have been called 'semi-brochs'.

The Roman interlude, AD 80 to c 430

From AD 43 south Britain became a province of the Roman Empire and, some forty years after, the Governor Agricola pushed north into Caledonia in a series of campaigns supported by the Roman fleet on the east coast, probably based on Cramond (Lothian) on the south shore of the Firth of Forth, where there was a Roman fort on the site occupied by the parish church. This action culminated in the defeat of the Caledonian tribes at the unknown site of Mons Graupius, probably near Stonehaven. Agricola then established a line of posts across the Forth-Clyde isthmus and a temporary legionary fortress at Inchtuthil (Tayside) on the river Tay, occupying 55 acres (22 ha) and accommodating over seven thousand men.

In 142 the line of posts was transformed into the Antonine Wall (named after the Emperor Antoninus Pius) by the then Governor, Lollius Urbicus; but it was never more than a temporary measure and was abandoned after forty years.

The wall stretched from Old Kilpatrick (Strathclyde) to Bo'ness (Lothian), a distance of 36 miles (58 km) but the best remains are to be seen in Central Region. It was 14 feet (4.3 m) wide and 10 or 12 feet (3.0-3.7 m) high, consisting of coursed sods faced with clay on a stone foundation, though east of Falkirk it was just clay. In front was a wide dry ditch of V-section with a line of upcast in front. It is a simpler and less effective wall than Hadrian's, without milecastle 'turrets'.

Behind ran a military way connected to a network of roads and some twenty forts from about 2 to 6 acres (0.8-2.4 ha) in area and placed about 2 miles (3 km) apart. All but one or two were of turf construction, as at Rough Castle near Bonnybridge (Central), a small 1 acre (0.4 ha) fort, with headquarters building, barracks and a bath-house annex. It is here that the wall is best seen.

Of other forts, the best known are Birrens (Dumfries and Galloway); Newstead (Borders) — on the trunk road from Corbridge to the wall — and Ardoch in Tayside. Cardean (Tayside) was the most northerly fort, beyond which was a line of marching camps reached across Grampian as far as the river Spey, for example Raedykes, a 90 acre (36 ha) one for ten thousand men.

Birrens was a 7 acre (2.8 ha) fort for less than a thousand men with headquarters, commandant's house, barracks, granaries and six surrounding ditches and ramparts. Nearby is Birrenswark Hill, on which is an iron age fort with two Roman siege encampments below, one with emplacements for siege engines.

An important stretch of road exists between Perth and Strageath with signal stations at intervals; at Summerston (Strathclyde) a stone-piered, probably trussed timber bridge crossed the Kelvin.

The early Christian period, c 400 to c 1070

Scotland was never occupied by the Romans and when in the fourth century, under Constantine, Christianity became the official religion of the Empire, St Ninian was the first to bring the new religion north with his mission of 397.

In Whithorn (Dumfries and Galloway) where he began, and therefore the oldest Christian site in Scotland, are the foundations of his original primitive fifth-century church of St Martin, the Candida Casa or White House, lying beneath a later medieval church. Its dry-stone walls were originally whitewashed.

In the sixth century St Columba arrived at Iona from Ireland, bringing a strong infusion of Celtic Christianity. This too became a famous mission base and from this time there are remains of Celtic monastic sites. At Eileach-an-Naoimh in the Garvellach Islands (Strathclyde) in the Firth of Lorne, the group of huts, church, refectory, guest-house, barns and other buildings must have been mostly of timber and wattle construction thatched with heather and turves. Later they were rebuilt in stone and from this phase are remains of underground cells and circular beehive huts of the Irish type, in which the roof is merely an extension of the walls.

Only the chapel can be definitely dated as early Celtic. It is small, 21 by 11 feet (6.4 by 3.4 m), and constructed of dry-stone walls converging into a corbelled roof. The floor is flagged and there is a single small east window with a double splay. There is also a double hut constructed and corbelled in the same way, one

8

cell being larger than the other. Most huts, however, were so small that a man would have to crouch to enter and could only stand upright in the middle. A dry-stone wall or 'cashel' enclosed the little settlement, the precursor of the precinct wall of the medieval monastery. Other monastic sites are known on Iona and Bute, and in Orkney and Shetland.

The Outer Hebrides have other examples of beehive huts. The little oratories or chapels of the period, too, are square-ended with converging side walls, both of which are Irish Celtic features, as at Chapel Finian (about AD 1000), a few miles west of Port William (Dumfries and Galloway), and the hermit's cell on Inchcolm in the Firth of Forth. The square east end of these diminutive oratories was destined to reach England via Northumbria and eventually, with Cistercian influence working in the same direction, was to oust the round apsidal end of the Latin churches to become the usual termination of the great churches of English medieval architecture.

Another Irish type of structure associated with monasteries is the tall, slender, slightly tapered detached tower, as at Brechin and Abernethy (Tayside). The first dates from about 1000 but is now built into the fabric of the medieval church. Its sculptured doorway has inclined jambs in the Irish manner but its roof is fourteenth-century. Abernethy tower is probably later and the upper storey appears to have been added in the twelfth century.

Viking colonisation took place from the ninth century on. Norse dwellings have been mentioned at Jarlshof: rectangular with rounded corners, they were built of earth with stone facing. Their timber roofs were supported on posts and turf-covered. Important remains are at Freswick (Highland) — with a steam bath — and at Birsay (Orkney).

Originally of the iron age and occupied until the ninth century is the hillfort of Dunadd (Strathclyde), fortress capital of Dalriada, the ancient kingdom of the Scots who migrated from Ireland in the sixth century and who were to give their name eventually to the whole country. Five stone-walled enclosures loop out from the fortified rocky summit and beyond these circles is a rampart.

There are other monuments of considerable merit and interest in the sculptured slabs of eastern Scotland, with their Pictish symbolism, and the high crosses of the west, such as Macmillan's, Kilmory Knap (Strathclyde), which constitute a fascinating field for the study of Celtic art. Sueno's Stone at Forres (Grampian) has vigorous figure sculpture while the beautifully carved seventh-century Ruthwell Cross (Dumfries and Galloway) is a masterpiece of sophisticated Northumbrian art. The Meigle Museum in Perth has a collection of local Christian stones which is one of the most remarkable in Europe.

2. Early medieval, c 1070 to c 1300

Romanesque, c 1070 to c 1200

On the marriage in about 1070 of Malcolm III (Ceanmore) to the saintly Margaret, of the Roman faith, Latin Christianity returned to oust or absorb the Celtic Church throughout Scotland, as it had already done in Northumbria in the seventh century. The Normans began to penetrate from the time they helped Queen Margaret's son Edgar in his struggle for the throne (1097) and when another son became King David I of Scotland in 1124. The Anglo-Norman prelates who came with them were imbued by the new continental spirit of reform and

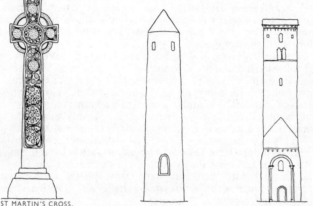

ST MARTIN'S CROSS, IONA   CELTIC ROUND TOWER   ROMANESQUE TOWER

familiar with a different and superior architectural tradition.

The austerity of the Celtic Church had always been unfavourable to architectural development but now a change of allegiance in religious forms and practices brought with it a European style, Romanesque, which had come to prevail over most of western Europe since the fall of the Roman Empire, and which had already developed regional variations in northern Italy, the Rhineland and France. Its two main sources were the remains of Roman architecture in the west, especially the early Christian churches of Italy, and the Byzantine style of the Eastern Empire centred on Constantinople.

The oldest Romanesque church in Scotland is the rude, greatly modified cell-chapel, only 26 by 10 feet (7.9 by 3.0 m), on Castle Rock, Edinburgh, built for Queen Margaret and which must date from before 1093, the year she died. The nave vault is modern but there is a vaulted semicircular apse within the square end. The typical twelfth-century church built by the lord as centre of the new ecclesiastical parish, which often coincided with his manor, was a small, unaisled building, compartmented in plan and consisting of two or three cells of diminishing size, the most easterly ending in a characteristic round aspe. Where Celtic influence lingered, however, the square east end was sometimes found, as at the primitive chapel or St Oran's, Iona (Strathclyde), or the two-cell chapel of St Mary on the island of Wyre (Orkney). St Mary's, Crosskirk (Highland), is a two-cell chapel with inclined jambs in the Irish manner.

The most complete and the finest Romanesque church in Scotland is at Dalmeny (Lothian). Small but beautiful in soft white stone, it is recognisably of the three-cell type consisting of a nave, chancel and apse. (The west tower is modern.) Window openings seem longer in their architectural frame but as usual are few, narrow and round-headed, being splayed to admit more light and formerly 'glazed' with oiled parchment or linen. The splendid south doorway is narrow and recessed and flanked by nook shafts, the round arch above being richly carved with strange animals and grotesques. The interior has ribbed quadri-partite vaulting of the period in the chancel and apse and the Norman chevron motif on the chancel arch. Above the doorway, outside, and in the nave is typical Romanesque interlaced wall arcading.

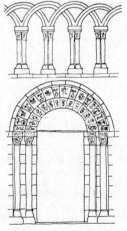

DALMENY CHURCH, DOORWAY

St Regulus' (or St Rule's) church, St Andrews (Fife), is a Romanesque church of about 1150, quite early by Scottish dating. It was probably a reliquary church to receive the remains of some early saint, possibly in the magnificent sarcophagus, about 900, still to be seen on the site. The later nave and sanctuary are gone and only the earlier parts survive: the short aisleless choir, which is narrow, high, and apsidal, and the very tall square tower. Most of the detailing is derived from a church at Wharram-le-Street and it appears to be the work of Yorkshire masons.

Leuchars (Fife) is later, has an apsidal sanctuary and shows well the Romanesque practice of using blind arcading, sometimes consisting of intersecting arches, as a system of wall decoration. The octagonal tower is seventeenth-century.

Interesting remains in the Orkneys are St Peter's on Birsay, a three-celled church with round apse; a church on Egilsay with a tall round western tower that resembles a Celtic refuge and a priest's house above its vaulted chancel; and St Nicholas's, Orphir, with round have and attached chancel, unique in Scotland. Built by an Orcadian crusader, it goes back, like the churches of the Knights Hospitallers, to the Holy Sepulchre in Jerusalem.

The great Anglo-Norman church was a much larger and more complex design. Cruciform in plan, it had an aisled nave and transepts to accommodate more eastern chapels at the same time as providing more light and abutment for the tower over the crossing. East ends were at first round — either of the ambulatory or of the parallel-apse type — but later became square. A section across the nave would show a main arcade, a gallery or triforium stage (at the level of the aisle roof) and a clerestory to light the nave. The great thickness of the wall necessitated massive piers and arches, and vertical wall shafts divided the elevations into bays. The nave was covered by a wooden ceiling under the roof, only the side aisles being vaulted as a rule. There was commonly a tower over the crossing and sometimes a pair of western towers. They would have had low pyramidal roofs.

St Magnus's Cathedral, Kirkwall (Orkney), was begun in 1137 when Orkney was a jarldom of the Norse Kingdom, but there is evidence that the masons were brought in from Durham, which had the most splendid of the great Anglo-Norman churches. Though modest in size — its nave is of seven bays, its choir of three — St Magnus's blunt massive forms express the Norman sense of power. The main arcade dominates the interior and its great round arches are carried on thick cylindrical piers like Durham. The capitals are simple without the incised ornament and decorative motifs of Durham, but the same weight, orderliness and monumentality are there. Originally the roof was of timber. The clerestory and vaulting are thirteenth-century — like the large rose window over the grouped lancets, a composition which is also an echo of Durham. The proportions of the interior, however, as in other great Scottish churches of the twelfth century, are narrow in relation to the height of the main vessel of the church.

The earliest monastic establishment, the Benedictine abbey of Dunfermline (Fife), was founded about 1074 by Queen Margaret, who may well have been married in the original church, a small rectangular building with a square western tower, on to which was built a square choir and round apse in the new Romanesque manner. The church which succeeded this about fifty years later is the present one: an aisled cruciform structure of which only the nave survives, the east end and transepts being replaced in the nineteenth century by a modern church which preserves the thirteenth-century shrine of St Margaret at its east end.

The thick-wall system of the Anglo-Norman style can be clearly seen, opened up into the three stages of the interior elevations, with great cylindrical piers, bold incised abstract ornament, cushion capitals and roll moulding in the centre of the arcade arches. The tall narrow proportions noted at Kirkwall are also there. The west front is late medieval, but early Romanesque in feeling, preserving a west doorway of that period (with side shafts and richly decorated orders) and also the idea of the twin flanking towers that were part of the original design. The tower with its spire and the extension to the north porch date as late as 1594 and are by James VI's Master of Works, William Schaw.

Nearby are the remains of a splendid royal palace, once the thirteenth-century guest-house of the monastery, and where Charles I was born. It is connected with the cloister by a vaulted gatehouse but only the undercroft and kitchen of the frater in the south range are to be seen, a striking early Gothic facade.

Kelso (Borders) — once the greatest of the border abbeys — had one of the most magnificent abbey churches in Scotland. Now there are few remains. The plan is cruciform with a central tower and with a western transept with a high tower over it, a scheme that goes back to the Carolingian cathedrals of the Rhineland and is found nowhere else in Scotland except at Kilwinning (Strathclyde). The external elevations are strong Romanesque designs of thick walls pierced by single round-arched windows and divided vertically by flat pilaster buttresses and horizontally by projecting string courses. Parts of the west front and a great west porch, perhaps a galilee (a penitents' chapel), are to be seen. The elevation of the north transept is

13

JEDBURGH ABBEY, CHOIR   JEDBURGH ABBEY, WEST FRONT

striking and is provided with a porch decorated with interlaced wall arcading and a lattice pattern in the triangular gable.

Though the nave piers are immense and carry enormous early Gothic arches, the general effect is livelier than outside. Above the nave arcade is a much lighter continuous line of smaller round arches borne on slender shafts. These stand forward from the main wall like a gallery or loggia and with their delicacy and quick rhythm make an attractive contrast with the ground base of the main arcade below. At the third stage the rhythm changes again, becoming more varied and emphatic.

The Augustinian order was the most numerous and influential in Scotland and of its houses, which included St Andrews and Holyrood, Jedburgh (Borders) founded by David I, was among the largest. The church was begun in 1130. Roofless now and ruinous, it had an aisled nave of nine bays, short transepts with a tower over the crossing, a choir of two bays and a presbytery beyond. The most immediately noticeable feature of the interior is the choir arcade, in which giant drum piers rise up through two-thirds of the elevation and support the richly carved arches of the triforium, and the nave arches spring from corbels half-way up the piers. The triforium arches are each further divided by two smaller arches springing from the cushion capital of the central shaft. This is the only example of this device in Scotland.

The clerestory above is galleried and is transitional to Gothic with its pointed arches. The nave shows a combination of Romanesque and Gothic elements, with its wide round slightly pointed arcade arches on boldly contoured compound piers, its triforium with two lancets and slender midshafts grouped below a broad Romanesque arch, and an early Gothic clerestory arcade of repeated pairs of solids and voids moving in rapid unbroken rhythm. But the Romanesque here has almost gone; the touch is lighter and more sensitive.

The west front is perhaps the best transitional example left in Scotland. The round-arched Norman doorway, with side shafts and recessed orders richly ornamented with chevron, billet moulding and bird's beak, is set in a slightly projecting porch topped by three gablets (reminiscent of Elgin, though much earlier), niched for statues. Above are tall round-arched windows, flanked by the remains of extremely slender lancet wall arcading, and a thirteenth-century Gothic rose window in the main gable. The whole composition, tall and narrow, is firmly held by the broad flat flanking buttresses with what were once octagonal finials.

The east front is still chiefly Romanesque and there are very fine Norman cloister doorways, richly carved. The massive tower over the crossing was rebuilt in the first years of the sixteenth century after the crossing piers had been replaced or strengthened. A chapel in line with the north transept and built in the same century is notable for its pointed barrel vault — a feature common in both secular and ecclesiastical buildings of the time — and for its traceried windows.

Early Gothic, c 1200 to c 1300

This new style, which originated in the Ile de France, was a complete structural system followed out logically so that from the crown of the high vault, via ribs, buttresses and piers, to the ground stress balanced stress in a carefully engineered skeleton of stone, in which walls were reduced to mere panels. Yet the Cistercians, who brought it to Britain, apparently missing the point of all this, still retained the Anglo-Norman thick wall, pierced it with the new lancets and simply used pointed arches and the slender shafts that went with them to articulate the surfaces in a new system of decoration.

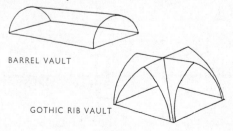

BARREL VAULT

GOTHIC RIB VAULT

This practice was to become characteristic of early Gothic in both England and Scotland and was no more than a superficial use of the elements of the style, at least until stone vaults became common and brought about a more thorough application of the Gothic system.

In the transepts at Dundrennan (Dumfries and Galloway) is typical mid twelfth-century Cistercian work resembling that of other abbeys in northern England. There is the same refined simplicity, the same use of round-arched windows, pointed arches and for the first time ribbed vaults over the transept chapels and the presbytery, a significant step forward in Scottish medieval architecture. Apart from the great doorway, the west front at Dundrennan is interesting for the corbels which once supported the roof of a narthex or porch with open arcades, like a section of cloister, the width of the front. This was a feature the Cistercians brought from Burgundy and its purpose was to serve as a galilee appropriated to penitents.

The chaper house south of the church dates from the late thirteenth century and belongs to the more elaborate form of Gothic known as 'Decorated'. The plan is rectangular with three aisles, and two rows of piers carry a ribbed vault. It is entered from the cloister through a richly ornamented doorway flanked by large pointed-arched openings, which make an interesting contrast with the older, plainer parts of the church.

At Restenneth Priory (Tayside) is a fine unaisled choir of the thirteenth century but of particular interest is its tall broach-spired tower, which in its lower portion appears to be Irish Celtic-Romanesque of about 1000 and was perhaps originally the tower of a narrow church of the Northumbrian type.

DORNOCH CATHEDRAL

Very few churches have come down unaltered so the early thirteenth-century Dunstaffnage Chapel (Strathclyde) in the so-called Early Pointed style is of particular note, especially in view of the refined quality of its rich detail, a remarkable discovery in so remote and austere a region. The plan is a single long narrow rectangle; walls are rubble with freestone dressings. There is an arched doorway of several orders in the south wall and both nave walls have two typical large lancet windows and one round-arched. Splays are wide internally and framed with moulded round arches supported by shafting. Another in Strathclyde is the thirteenth-century St Brendan's Chapel adjoining Skipness Castle, with typical long narrow Scottish proportions. Dornoch Cathedral (Highland) dates from 1224 but its beautiful golden fabric was much restored in the Early Pointed style in the nineteenth century.

The two great secular churches of the early Gothic period in Scotland are the cathedrals of Glasgow, the best preserved cathedral on the Scottish mainland, and Elgin, regrettably ruinous.

Glasgow was raised over the shrine of St Mungo (or Kentigern) and this determines the plan, with a square-ended ambulatory allowing pilgrims to circulate. Above the large and outstanding crypt at the east end, with its beautiful elaborate vaulting of the first half of the thirteenth century, are an aisled choir and a presbytery, extending westwards through short transepts and an aisled eight-bay nave, with a fine reconstructed fourteenth-century flat timber roof, to what was once a two-tower west front. Over the crossing is a central tower with early fifteenth-century spire. Other fifteenth-century features of exceptional interest are a chapter house with a richly carved entrance, the aisle of Archbishop Blackadder, a 'castellated' sacristy, and a fine stone screen or pulpitum. The total effect is surprisingly unified.

Elgin Cathedral (Grampian) was begun in 1224 and built in the early Gothic style. In 1390 it was burnt and in the fifteenth century reconstructed. A contrast between the two building periods may be seen by comparing the single lancets of the eastern elevation with the large traceried windows in the south wall. This may well have been the most beautiful Gothic building in all Scotland, with hints of early French influence.

The aisled choir is comparatively well preserved. This is a splendid early Gothic composition complete with rose window in the gable and flanked by octagonal turrets, terminating in pinnacles, into which bands of arcaded niches have been cut, two below and one above.

The west front is high and impressive in its simple dignity of proportion but it also displays some striking features: the elaborately shafted and moulded west doorway divided into two portals with a sculptured tympanum and, above, three niched gablets, and a large fifteenth-century traceried window. Inside, over the west doorway is an arcaded passage which is similar to others at the border abbeys, at Holyrood, and especially at Arbroath. The chapter house is almost complete, a thirteenth-century octagonal chamber vaulted from a central pier. The windows are later.

The centrally planned chapter house, like those at Elgin, Holyrood and the thirteenth-century Priory of Inchcolm in the Firth of Forth, is based on a unique English tradition found nowhere else in Europe. At Inchcolm too there is a small but complete cloister. St Andrews Cathedral (priory) in Fife, once the metropolitan cathedral served by Augustinian canons, is largely early Gothic. The sequence of the eastern range of the large cloister can be studied clearly; slype, chapter house, warming house (now an excellent museum), with dorter over. The 'mantle' or precinct wall is the finest in Scotland. It is a late example of early sixteenth-century date, high and furnished with round towers with gun loops, but it is based on an earlier wall. The Pends is the vaulted passage of a fourteenth-century gatehouse sited to the west of the church.

Holyrood, now apparently a Renaissance palace, was once one of the most splendid abbeys of medieval Scotland. The thirteenth-century nave, buttressed outside by a series of deep Gothic buttresses of diminishing stages and now fore-shortened by the introduction of a seventeenth-century 'Gothic' window, has a graceful arcade and was vaulted throughout. The west front has an impressive recessed doorway and plentiful wall arcading, especially in two tiers on each side of the flanking towers, of which only one remains. Behind the large traceried windows with flattened arches is a tribune or galilee. Unfortunately, the east end and the cloistral buildings were swept away to make room for the sixteenth-century palace.

The only large Premonstratensian house in Scotland was Dryburgh (Borders), founded in the twelfth century by the Constable of Scotland. What is left of the interior elevations shows two interesting features. The first is a tendency to squeeze out the middle one of the three stages in favour of the upper one, by reducing the triforium to little more than a series of quatrefoil openings. The second is an unusual emphasis on verticality gained by the use of prominent wall shafting, rather than allowing the horizontals more prominence, as was usual. The building stone — a lovely warm rose colour — is of exceptional quality. In the east range the unaisled barrel-vaulted chapter house is separated from the church by sacristy, library and inner parlour and is succeeded by a large warming house, a slype to the

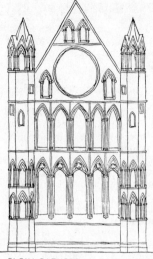

ELGIN CATHEDRAL, EAST END

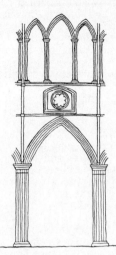

DRYBURGH ABBEY, NORTH TRANSEPT

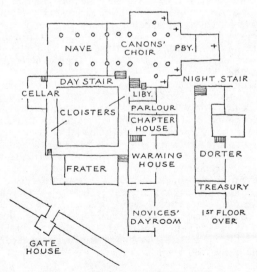

DRYBURGH ABBEY

19

infirmary and an aisled hall. Above these rooms at first-floor level ran the dorter, reached by a day stair next to the chapter house: at one end were the night stairs down into the transept, at the other the reredorter. The undercroft of the frater remains in the south range; but there was never any west range at all - only a wall.

Arbroath Abbey (Tayside), largely completed by the early thirteenth century, was a Tironensian house colonised from Kelso. The west front has two massive towers of Tironensian proportions and a recessed Norman doorway with a tribune above. Here the doorway projects to support it and it is the most elaborate of all, for it has become a pillared hall more than a passage, opening to the outside through three pointed arches under gablets and to the church through a graceful pointed arcade. It has been, possibly, the most impressive feature of its kind in Britain. Above it shone an immense rose window the full width of the wall.

The south transept is well preserved, with enormous lancets, above which is another smaller rose window. As at Kelso, the interior walls are elaborated with galleries and wall arcading that are exceptions to the ideal of restrained simplicity. There is another show of enrichment in the form of twelfth-century wall arcading on the lower stages of the western towers, a subtle display of visual rhythms. The high sacristy, vaulted and very well preserved, is typical of the fifteenth century and contains an interesting treasury chamber.

There are Tironensian houses at Lindores (Fife) and at Kilwinning (Strathclyde), which has a south transept with lancet windows and chapels, and a chapter house of considerable distinction.

Coldingham Priory (Borders), a cell of the Benedictine cathedral-monastery of Durham, has a slender choir, now in use again, a two-storey design with pairs of round-arched windows below and pairs of lancets above making it of late twelfth-century to early thirteenth-century date. The lower part of the inside elevation has a lively unbroken run of pointed arcading with vesicas and quatrefoils in the spandrels. Above, the clerestory arcade has a different rhythm with the lancet arches over the window openings carried on two-tiered clustered shafts giving additional height and greater accent at certain intervals. Though the foliate capitals are a little heavy-handed the total effect of the scheme is rather delicate and most pleasing. Once more it shows the Britsh tendency to treat the structural forms of early Gothic more as a system of applied sculptural decoration to articulate a wall surface.

3. Castellated, c 1070 to c 1500

Medieval castles

Architectural works of any size or number are not to be found before the twelfth century, when the kingdom of Scotland under the early Canmore kings was rapidly becoming transformed into a feudal state on the Anglo-Norman pattern. The administrative centres and strongholds of the new feoffs, thrown up in remarkably short time and in considerable numbers, were the 'motte and bailey' castles.

They are most numerous in south-west Scotland, especially in the long dales where many of the earlier grants were obtained; but there are many in Grampian, where they were imitated by the Celtic chiefs when they were drawn into the new feudal system, of which the castles were the effective symbol.

This most characteristic fortification consists essentially of a motte or mound with an adjacent enclosure, both of which were surrounded by a fosse and palisade of squared timbers, the mound crowned with a timber tower and reached from the bailey by a flying bridge of timber over the inner fosse, a wet or dry ditch. Unless later translated into stone, such structures leave behind only their earthworks, albeit sometimes large ones, as evidence of their former existence. Huntly, Castle Duffus (both Grampian) and Castle Urquhart (Highland) are all stone castles erected on earlier motte and bailey sites, the first two on an impressive scale, the last an interesting example of a double bailey. At Duffus the wide outer fosse encloses as much as 8 acres (3.2 ha). The tower on the motte was the ultimate strong point and the bailey was often large enough to contain additional timber buildings such as a hall, perhaps with a kitchen at one end and a solar or lord's private chamber at the other, a chapel, and shelter for the dependants and their stock in time of danger.

The English development of the motte and bailey castle into a 'keep and bailey' castle in the twelfth century is rare in Scotland and the normal successor of the motte and bailey castle is the thirteenth-century stone castle of 'enceinte', or enclosure of high embattled curtain wall.

The earliest stone castles are two remarkable remains from the twelfth century, when the peripheral regions were controlled by Norse jarls and enjoyed a relative prosperity. Cobbie Row's Castle on the island of Wyre in the Orkneys is the *steinkastala* or stone castle mentioned in the *Orkneyinga Saga* as being built about 1145; it is a small keep, about 20 feet (6 m) square, built with great skill from the local flagstone. Originally it was probably a building of two or three storeys, with a saddleback roof, its openings just narrow slits, entered on the first floor by means of an outside stair or a ladder. Surrounding the tower was a circular rampart and fosse.

Perhaps Castle Sween in Strathclyde is even earlier, though still twelfth-century. This is a larger trapezoid structure with large but shallow angle buttresses and buttresses of the pilaster type in the centre of each wall. There is a sea-gate but the main entrance is through a round-arched door in one of these mid-wall buttresses and apart from these there are no other openings in the wall. A stone stair on the right of the entrance led to the parapeted wall walk. Despite the comparative breadth of the plan the whole area was evidently floored and roofed and it was not a courtyard castle but a keep. Both castles have later additions.

Rothesay (Bute, Strathclyde) appears to have been a twelfth-century circular shell keep on a flat-topped motte which in the early thirteenth century was given four round towers outside the wall and a forework to protect the entrance. The original walls, still 30 feet (9 m) tall, were raised about 1500, when the larger forework (combining entrance, great hall and barbican) and small postern were added, and in such a way as to preserve the original battlements like a fossil in the new wall, complete with putlog holes for the hoarding or overhanging gallery. Within the bailey were domestic buildings and a chapel and outside the curtain and wide berm was a deep wet moat so that the general appearance now is that of a tiny but regular castle of enceinte. The circular plan is found nowhere else in Scotland.

The finest Scottish castles of enceinte are equipped with mural towers like Rothesay but many were not conceived as more than curtain walls in the first place. The thirteenth-century enclosure of Balvenie (Grampian), a castle of the Comyns (Balliol's supporters against Bruce) and one of the largest and best preserved in the north, is quadrangular, the normal shape, and is surrounded by a massive wall of rubble, brought at intervals to level courses by pinnings, and a ditch cut out of the rock. The rubble technique was not usual in castles of enceinte and the general practice was to employ dressed ashlar masonry. Most of the later buildings at Balvenie are of the fifteenth and sixteenth centuries and there is an excellent example of a yett, a strong iron 'trellis' gate of interpenetrating bars used to protect entrance doorways, a most effective means of defence with a similar role to that of the more orthodox portcullis. It is a notable Scottish feature.

Another mainland castle of this kind is Loch Doon (Strathclyde), re-erected on its present site, but once on an island in the lock. Well preserved, if affords much information about the features of the period, for example the form of simple entrance with pointed archway and portcullis and drawbars to protect and

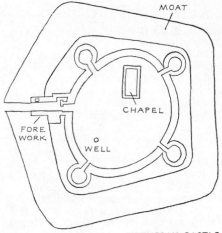

ROTHESAY CASTLE

secure the door. The quality of the masonwork is exceptionally high. Typical of the time is the batter or spread given to the bases of the towers to protect them.

A most interesting group of curtain-wall castles, dating from the thirteenth century and associated with the struggle to overthrow Norse power in the Hebrides, occurs on the west coast: they occupy rocky sites by the sea and are small and irregular in plan. On an island in Loch Moidart is Castle Tioram, Ardnamurchan (Highland), where the restricted site has produced a shape which is only roughly pentagonal. The outside corners of the curtain are rounded and the entrance is little more than a narrow opening (with lattice work above), both of which features are typical of this closely related group of castles. The entrance is projected by a passage into the courtyard, and over it a stone stair leads to the wall-head. Mingarry, also in Ardnamurchan, offers an example of the same type; but Kisimul on Barra in the Western Isles has a square keep which is set in the curtain wall. Dunstaffnage (Strathclyde) has a quadrangular enceinte and round towers. Dating from the thirteenth century, it still preserves one tower as a keep and in this sense may be regarded as transitional to the concentric castle of Edwardian type which represents the climax of this development in fortification. Nearby is a chapel which, though in ruins, is a good specimen of early Gothic ecclesiastical architecture.

Inverlochy (Highland) is also quadrangular in plan with four round towers at the angles. The symmetry of the design is remarkable and classic, though one of the towers — larger than the others — is again retained as a keep or donjon. There was a wet moat filled from the river and a water gate as well as a main entrance of the single type.

The great concentric castles of Scotland are similar in many ways to the Edwardian castles of North Wales. Deriving, via the Crusades, from Byzantine examples, the typical thirteenth-century castle has its defences arranged in a concentric system of parapeted curtain walls punctuated at intervals by towers, square or round, projecting from the face of the curtain so as to command its face. The entrance has now expanded into a massive twin-towered gatehouse and in the classic form the keep has disappeared altogether, its functions having become absorbed in the new gatehouse.

Bothwell (Strathclyde), reconstructed in 1331-7 by John de Kilburne, one of the earliest known master masons, despite its late date still retains the concept of the keep for, besides the normal polygonal curtain with towers and gatehouse, there is a massive cylindrical donjon of fine ashlar enriched with Gothic detail in a manner appropriate to its scale. The entrance to the keep is at ground level but is ingeniously protected. On the first floor is the octagonal lord's hall with imitation timber vaulting carried on a central timber pier. Elsewhere, in the mural chambers and passages, pointed barrel vaults with applied ribs are used. The castle changed hands many times during the War of Independence and in 1337 half the donjon was thrown into the river. When it was subsequently restored it was, unfortunately, replaced by a straight wall. At other angles of the enceinte are round towers, with square towers intermediately placed, and a main gatehouse later demolished. A hall and chapel were added within the bailey in the fourteenth century, and, in the fifteenth century, machicolations.

Kildrummy (Grampian) also has hall and chapel closely associated and placed near one of the angle towers. But here the chapel with its triple lancets on first-floor level breaches the curtain in a most irrational way. The largest tower in the enceinte, remote from the entrance, is retained as a donjon, and it has a superb gatehouse, about 1290, of the type associated with Edward I's master mason, James of St George. With its massive twin drum towers it is now the strongest and largest structure in the design and is pushed out towards the field in a new offensive manner at variance with the old idea of a castle as a purely defensive work. From now on it is to serve as both military and domestic accommodation, apart from the bailey buildings. In this way it came to supersede the keep and to acquire the title of keep-gatehouse. An interesting feature is the barbican complete with drawbridge pit. The plan is roughly pentagonal with four towers, apart from the gatehouse: two round, of which one is the donjon, and two round to the field and square to the bailey. It is the most complete thirteenth-century secular building in Scotland despite the later work of the fifteenth and sixteenth centuries.

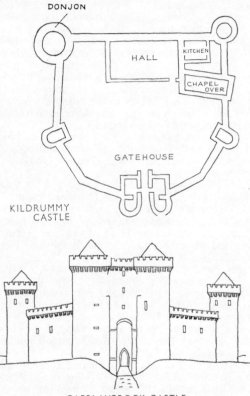

CAERLAVEROCK CASTLE

Caerlaverock (Dumfries and Galloway), on the shore of the Solway Firth, dates from the mid thirteenth century and still retains its unusual triangular plan magnificently expressed in its high walls and great towers: two round ones at the base angles and a splendid twin-towered keep-gatehouse with rib-vaulted hall at the apex, the earliest example of such a structure in Scotland. The machicolated wall-heads are fifteenth-century.

At Dirleton (Lothian) the rocky outcrop on which the castle is sited restricted the plan and resulted in a much tighter scheme. The small bailey is almost an adjunct to a cluster of three towers (that might be described as a 'clustered donjon') which are pushed forward to cover the entrance in the aggressive manner of the keep-gatehouse and are the principal element of defence and also provide accommodation, in two polygonal vaulted halls (one above the other) for the castellan on the first floor and the garrison below. There are two more mural towers in the curtain and a fifteenth-century hall over cellarage, with a kitchen at one end and apartments at the other. There is a pit prison.

In the earlier middle ages, before the arrival of the tower house, which was destined virtually to monopolise secular building, fortified manor houses of the hall type were probably not uncommon, though only a few examples have survived. Morton (Dumfries and Galloway) and Rait (Highland) show the type: a rectangular hall, to which a round tower has been attached, raised on an undercroft and roofed with a saddle roof within a crenellated parapet. The earlier work at Hailes Castle (Lothian) is of an intermediate type.

The War of Independence of the first part of the fourteenth century interrupted castle building. This was rather a time of siege and demolition than of construction and development. The largest works begun afterwards are the first to show a new influence in castle and design. The lord's retinue, retained both to protect and to further his personal ambitions, had to be accommodated within his walls but separate from his quarters.

Tantallon, perched dramatically on the coast of Lothian, is one of these 'livery and maintenance' castles of this period. Behind an immense curtain wall, later reinforced against firearms, that cuts across the neck of the promontory a second hall has been provided below the great hall for the specific purpose of accommodating the garrison whilst the great gatehouse that occupies the centre of the curtain contains the domestic quarters of the castellan.

Only through this entrance could the castle be entered and it was securely controlled by the lord himself. The very high curtain was flanked by tall round towers of considerable strength, and the whole strength of the defence has been massed at the front: there is really only one section of curtain wall. This was made possible by the nature of the site, which falls away in sheer 100 foot (30 m) cliffs on all sides except one, but that this aggressive posture was more generally adopted about this time can be shown by reference to Doune (Central).

Doune was designed for Regent Albany (though probably intended to be extended later) in the last years of the fourteenth century and restored in 1883. It shows the principles of forward

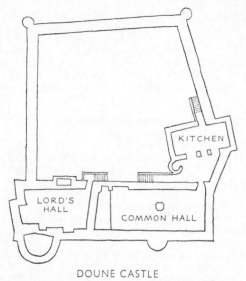

DOUNE CASTLE

construction and separation of accommodation and also marks the final disappearance of the donjon and gatehouse. Within the main block at the front of the castle are halls for the garrison and for the lord, both on the first floor but insulated and served by separate stairs from the courtyard. The lord's accommodation lies above the passage entrance, which tunnels through the main frontal mass. The curtain walls are 40 feet (12 m) high and have open bartizans or projecting turrets at the angles and mid-wall positions too. The parapets, however, do not overhang and machicolations have disappeared, except over the postern.

One of the most individual medieval castles in Britain, Ravenscraig, stands sadly neglected on a promontory on the coast of Fife. Firearms were first used against the Scots by Edward III in 1327 and Ravenscraig was the first British castle to be systematically designed as an artillery fort from the beginning of its construction in 1460: it antedates Henry VIII's coastal forts by some eighty years. The plan resembles Tantallon, but the principal apartments are in the two massive round flanking towers or bastions, one serving as a tower house dwelling, the other presumably for the garrison. The frontal range has a passage entrance and vaulted basements with inverted keyhole gun ports and, above, an open gun platform with breastwork and wide-mouthed embrasures. Walls are specially thickened across the front to withstand cannon shot and the towers (and perhaps

27

the parapet too) had wall-heads that sloped back. These features, together with rounded parapets and a general lowering of height, were to be the means of resisting attack by ordnance.

At Stirling Castle a comparison of the fifteenth-century gate-house with the early eighteenth-century outwork of batteries shows in sharp contrast the ideas governing fortifications before and after the use of ordnance.

Tower houses

In the second part of the fourteenth century, the other principal secular structures to be erected were tower houses, a type of castellated architecture that combined the functions of keep and manor house, arranged vertically instead of horizontally as in the English way. The type is found nowhere else, for the pele of the English border, coming late as it did, appears to be an imitation of the tower house. It lasted for some three hundred years and even today several hundred are extant.

The tower house was the most economic stronghold that the lairds could devise, effective as a localised centre of defence and adapted to domestic needs and social pride. Moreover the insecurity and unsettled conditions in Scotland caused the 'house of fence' to continue right into the seventeenth century.

The earliest tower houses of the fourteenth century are square or rectangular in plan with thick plain walls, often constructed of fine ashlar, rising to a crenellated parapet with perhaps angle turrets. Early parapets are flush or project only slightly. Above a low stone-vaulted basement with ventilation slits and a trap to the first floor was a high vault divided by a timber floor, resting on corbels or 'scarcements', into a great hall on the first floor and a solar over. Higher again were one or two more storeys under the saddle-back roof, pitched low and covered with stone slate. The entrance was on the first or second floor, protected by strong drawbars, and was reached by a timber stair outside or a retractable ladder; openings are generally small, rectangular and chamfered. Internally a wheel or spiral stair was contained in the thickness of a corner of the wall, sometimes being transferred from one corner to another in order to break the run of the stair. Eventually it terminates at the wall-head in a cap house.

Despite the superficial resemblance to the Norman keep the influence cannot be direct for tower houses differ in certain important respects: they lack a forebuilding, cross wall and pilaster buttresses, and have barrel vaults where there would have been timber floors above. Where there are timber floors there are no mid supports such as the Anglo-Normans used.

Loch Leven (Tayside) is a good early specimen although the polygonal curtain wall and the round angle tower are probably sixteenth-century, as the gun loops show. Its early date is suggested by the absence of wall chambers, the scarcity of stairs and the unusual height of the main entrance on the second floor. As this simple type continued to be built, an early date cannot always be inferred.

On an island in the river Dee in Dumfries and Galloway stands the grim Douglas stronghold of Threave Castle, another splendid example of five storeys with a barmkin (courtyard) wall, formerly with angle towers, which also date from the sixteenth century, about the time of Flodden, though this feature can also be earlier. Entrance to the tower was on the second floor by a timber bridge from an upper floor of the gatehouse in the curtain opposite, while the wall tops appear to have carried permanent timber hoarding.

Drum (Grampian) is a classic early tower house with an exceptional early parapet. Crichton (Lothian) and Hallforest (Grampian) are other examples.

The later fourteenth century saw an attempt to obtain more accommodation by adding a 'jam' or wing to the main structure, thus giving it an L-shaped plan. Since there need not be a correspondence of levels between the two wings of the tower house more storeys of lower chambers could be obtained from the jam. The position of the entrance was also modified for the door could now be conveniently situated on the ground floor as it was possible to give it protection in the re-entrant angle between the main tower and the jam. In this case the main stair could be placed in the jam, and perhaps the kitchen or guardroom with bedrooms above. Above first-floor level, access might be by a stair turret in the re-entrant angle.

At first the jam was rather short, as may be seen at Craigmillar Castle (Edinburgh), where the large L-plan tower is the nucleus. Craigmillar grew by addition into a rectangular courtyard scheme. The doorway is approached from the gateway by a devious exposed route and was protected by a drawbridge. The great hall had a handsome fireplace in the gable flanked by stone-benched embrasured windows at the dais end and a screen at the other. There is a high curtain wall of the fifteenth century with angle towers (machicolated in the manner of the period) and making what resembles an earlier enceinte. Against the east and west walls were erected further buildings and around the whole in the sixteenth century was thrown an outer curtain. In the second half of the seventeenth century the west range was rebuilt in a Renaissance manner. Castle Campbell (Central) developed similarly.

The L-plan remains one of the commonest plans of Scottish tower houses. Another means at this time of obtaining more accommodation and particularly greater privacy was to 'borrow' space from the walls in the form of small mural chambers and garderobes. This, together with an increased provision of wheel stairs, is another development of the late fourteenth century but one which reaches its fullest extent in the next.

Affleck (Tayside) is a smaller L-plan tower house of four storeys noted for the exceptional elaboration of its internal arrangements and the small but distinguished solar, off which opens an oratory or little chapel. The rubble walls are rendered with harl but the masonwork and detailing are exceptionally fine. Cardoness (Dumfries and Galloway) is a similar small tower where the fireplaces and aumbries are a special feature. Decorated with Gothic ornament, these became part of the general trend of the fifteenth century that includes a liberal use of heraldic decoration and barrel vaults to which purely ornamental ribs have been applied by way of embellishment.

Both Comlongon (Dumfries and Galloway) and Elphinstone Tower (Lothian) are fine massive fifteenth-century tower houses where the upper part of the walls especially are ingeniously hollowed out into mural chambers and where there is most generous provision of stairs. Both have kitchen recesses at the lower end of the great hall.

Another feature of this period is larger windows with wider embrasures and at Borthwick (Lothian) an oratory is accommodated in one. This great tower house, still occupied and dating from 1430, is an incomparable example of the form; not only in its unusual plan, with two jams over 100 feet (30 m) high projecting from the same side of the main structure and overshadowing the space between, but also in its scale and the general distinction of the planning. Over ground-floor cellarage the great hall is reached by an entrance passage to the 'screens' at first floor level. The kitchen is in one jam, with the solar (with a large garderobe) in the other, all at the same level. The hall has a plastered and painted, pointed barrel vault, deep embrasured windows, a large fireplace with a fine canopy, supported by squat columns, and a buffet cupboard. There is also a canopied basin in the 'screens', over which there is a gallery.

Above the hall is the great chamber with the oratory and two more floors of further rooms above that, each one being barrel-vaulted. In the wings are more bedrooms and servants' quarters while a series of wheel stairs and straight flights both serve separately and connect the jams and the main block.

Borthwick is exceptionally well built. The masonry work, both in the 12 foot (3.7 m) thick walls — where there are few narrow windows and the stones are carefully graded from base to wall-head — and in the detailing, is of very high quality. The top of the towers is finished by a heavily machicolated parapet, which boldy oversails in the late medieval style, and stone-slabbed roof. There is also a later curtain wall with two round

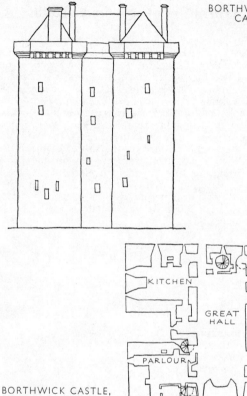

BORTHWICK
CASTLE

KITCHEN

GREAT
HALL

PARLOUR

BORTHWICK CASTLE,
FIRST FLOOR

towers, one a massive drum gatehouse designed to protect the outer entrance. The route to the tower entrance is circuitous and involves a bridge from the curtain, as at Threave. The curtain wall is pierced with gun loops.

4. Late Gothic, c 1350 to c 1500

Churches and abbeys

During the first three-quarters of the fourteenth century, which opened with the War of Independence and continued with the bitter struggle that ebbed and flowed across the turbulent border, a great many early medieval castles and churches were destroyed, including Jedburgh and Melrose abbeys.

However a number of parish churches date from this period, a notable group occurring in the relative security of Fife. St Monans is perhaps the best, a well preserved, well proportioned gem of the fourteenth century on the shores of the Firth of Forth. Small, with choir and transepts but no nave, it was originally a Dominican friars' church though the other buildings of the friary have disappeared. Over the transepts is a broad tower finished with a stumpy spire with spirelights. The interior is very well lit from relatively large windows with curvilinear tracery of the period.

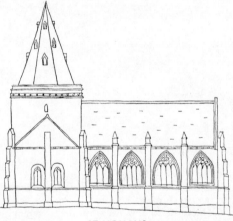

ST MONANS

The fourteenth century is the century of the Decorated form of Gothic, so styled because of its characteristic love of elaboration compared with the more restrained style of First Pointed Gothic. This elaboration may take the form of an abundance of applied ornament to vaults and structural members, and the adoption in particular of various curved forms and motifs. The curvilinear tracery noted at St Monans is one of the

1. (Left) Ruthwell Cross, Dumfries and Galloway.
2. (Right) Sueno Stone, Forres, Grampian.

3. (Left) The Round Tower, Abernethy, Tayside.

4. (Right) The Round Tower, Brechin, Tayside.

5. The church at Leuchars, Fife.

6. The church at Dalmeny, Lothian.

7. Dunfermline Abbey, Fife.

8. The west front, Jedburgh Abbey, Borders.

9. Dundrennan Abbey, Dumfries and Galloway.

10. The west front, Elgin Cathedral, Grampian.

11. *Dryburgh Abbey, Borders.*

12. *St Andrews Abbey, Fife.*

13. *The palace block, Huntly Castle, Grampian.*

14. The north range, Crichton Castle, Lothian.

15. Caerlaverock Castle, Dumfries and Galloway.

16. The church at St Monans, Fife.

17. *Sweetheart Abbey (New Abbey), Dumfries and Galloway.*

18. *Melrose Abbey, Borders.*

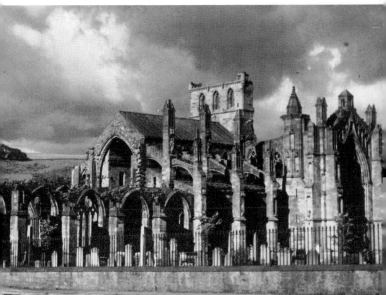

19. *Roslin Chapel, Lothian.*

20. *Crossraguel Abbey, Strathclyde.*

21. St Giles' Cathedral, Edinburgh.

22. Glamis Castle, Tayside.

23. Linlithgow Palace, Lothian.

24. Falkland Palace, Fife: the gatehouse tower.

25. Kinneil House, near Bo'ness, Central Region.

26. The Binns, near Linlithgow, Lothian.

hallmarks of the Decorated style. The ogee arch of double curvature is also typical, especially the 'nodding' ogee which produces not only a greater richness of carved decoration but also sinuosity and three-dimensional rippling movements in the forms themselves.

Dunblane Cathedral (Central), with its west front of tall lancets over a central doorway, dates from the thirteenth century and even earlier in the lower part of the tower which it incorporates, but there is much rich early Decorated work in the nave arcade, and the east end. The design is unusual in that there are no transepts and there is an uninterrupted view down the whole length of the nave. The long narrow proportions are in the recognisable Scottish manner.

Fortrose (Highland) is a ruined red-sandstone cathedral which has much fourteenth-century work especially in the vaulted south aisle, where there is some exceptional detail of the period.

New Abbey (Dumfries and Galloway), known as Sweetheart Abbey since it was founded in memory of John Balliol, whose heart lies on his wife's breast before the high altar, is now a ruin, but very considerable portions remain including the full height of the nave, the transepts, the tower over the crossing, and a short aisleless choir. The west front once had a narthex for this was a Cistercian house colonised from Dundrennan, the last founded in Scotland.

Melrose (Borders), the first Cistercian house in Scotland, was founded nearly a hundred and fifty years before the present structure, which dates from about 1385. The large and complex general plan of the monastery is typically Cistercian, with an additional cloister for the conversi insulated from the choir monks' cloister by a 'lane'. Both cloisters are laid out north of the church, towards the river Tweed, as was usual if the drainage of the site required it. There is a fine example, too, of a monastic drain and a lade which worked the abbey mill.

Extensive remains include windows, rib vaulting, rich arcading and carved detail (including open quatrefoil parapet, nodding ogees and much interesting sculpture), all in the Decorated and later styles, which contrast sharply with the severity of the fragments of its Romanesque predecessor incorporated in the lower parts of the west front. Along the south side of the church are two splendid sets of flying buttresses conducting the thrust of the high vault over both aisles, the only medieval flying buttresses in Scotland designed at the outset to fulfil a structural purpose.

The splendid chapter house was a large three-aisled rectangle with ribbed vault, whilst opposite the great frater, which is set at right angles to the cloister, was an unusually fine laver or washing place. An excellent site museum has been made from the Commendator's House. The barrel vault over the west end of the nave dates from 1618, when it was clumsily converted into a Protestant church.

Though dating about 1450, the most highly decorated building in Scotland is Roslin Chapel (Lothian), once the Collegiate Church of St Matthew though never completed; what remains is a small but lofty choir with low aisles and chapels. The decoration is astonishingly profuse, with elaborate stone traceries, intricate leaf patterns on the aisle vaulting, and abundantly carved piers. Flying buttresses are used merely as decorative devices. Some of the detail in the choir has been compared with Portuguese work, which has a similar oriental richness. This kind of ornamentation is only explicable as an exotic extravaganza representing the peculiar taste of the Earl of Orkney, who employed foreign craftsmen to realise it.

The more typical church of this period was a quite different conception. The collegiate churches which were the new expressions of medieval piety were the headquarters of colleges of secular canons, priests whose work was not to separate themselves from the laity but to minister to them. Such a church might be parochial or a special foundation such as a chantry church. In Scotland the finest of these churches was Lincluden (Dumfries and Galloway), dating from the late fourteenth century. The choir (the nave was never built) is closed to the west by a stone rood screen with a central doorway crowned with elaborate sculpture in a large arched recess. The interior of the choir is, despite its decay, a splendid example of the Decorated style and contains much heraldic ornament and the magnificent fifteenth century tomb of Margaret Douglas. This is incorporated into the design as were the canopied sedilia and piscina.

At Dunglas (Lothian) the Collegiate Church, one of the earliest in Scotland, is in a much better condition. It was an aisleless cruciform church with a sacristy opening off the north side of the choir and a central tower of three storeys. There are also fine sedilia with ornately carved canopies. Though small, this is an impressive church with a rich interior. The roofs are stone-vaulted with heavy stone slabs outside, overlapping alternately to give the appearance of broad, square channelling with a broken ridge line. This provides a most effective roof covering with a sturdy, rugged-textured finish; it seems to be a wholly Scottish invention, one of those which reflect the national spirit of independence in the late Gothic period.

Another example of it may be seen at Corstorphine Collegiate Church, in Edinburgh, where the low crouching structure is finished with an effective roof of massive stone slabs and a tower with short, blunt spire. The interior is unspoiled, with fine sedilia and tombs: most old Scottish kirks lost much of their original

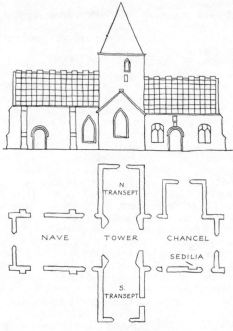

DUNGLASS, COLLEGIATE CHURCH

interiors after the Reformation.

The Collegiate Church of Seton (Lothian) was intended to be cruciform in plan (though yet again the nave was probably never built) with a tower and broach spire designed to stand over the crossing. The broach spire is a form more usually associated with early Gothic though here it appears in a blunter version. Significantly the apse to the choir is three-sided, another feature of late Gothic churches in Scotland. The interior has stone vaulting, good window tracery and the arched recess of the mural tomb (paralleled in the transepts at Dunglass), a monument to the Lord Seton who was killed at Flodden Field.

Tullibardine Chapel (Tayside) was one of the few collegiate churches in Scotland to be completed. Its open timber roof and mouldings are of high quality and an external feature which is characteristically Scottish — albeit more usually found in houses — is the crow-stepped or 'corbie' gable. The west end was fortified and has the addition of a small tower.

The fourteenth-century Collegiate Church of St Duthus, Tain

(Highland), has interesting fenestration whilst that at Arbuth-nott (Grampian) dates from the thirteenth century, but the most striking part is the massively buttressed and vaulted fifteenth-century Arbuthnott Aisle and polygonal chapel. Restalrig Collegiate Church, Portobello (Lothian), has an interesting fifteenth-century hexagonal pilgrimage shrine under the royal chapel. Bothwell (Strathclyde) is another example and Crichton (Lothian) has barrel vaulting and an interesting tower and bellcote.

In the later middle ages there was an increase in the size and wealth of towns and one reflection was the remodelling of many parochial churches, which were made larger, more elaborate, and were better lit from wider windows. Thus at Borthwick (Lothian) an aisle roofed with a barrel vault was added to what was originally a Romanesque church with an apsidal east end.

St Michael's, Linlithgow (Lothian) dates mainly from the fifteenth and early sixteenth centuries. Its four-square simplicity and sparse decoration are characteristically Scottish, as are the crow-stepped gables and the separate gable roofs of transept and porch. Its open crown spire was demolished in the early nineteenth century. The five-sided apse is a remarkable example of the later type of apse. The interior once had a timbered ceiling but the predominant impression is one of austere simplicity.

The Church of the Holy Rude, Stirling, has a fine open timber roof with attractive piers of blue and white stones. Its late Gothic polygonal apse is five-sided like St Michael's.

St Mary's, Haddington (Lothian), is now roofless apart from the nave but enough of its cruciform extensions in transepts and choir remain to confirm that this was one of the largest and finest fifteenth-century parish churches, It is very English in general aspect but its windows show some of the best Scottish late Gothic tracery patterns and are of a type which runs parallel to those of the later period of French Gothic and which is known as 'flamboyant' from their fluttering, flame-like shapes. They are a reminder that the 'Auld Alliance' with France was to have cultural influences. A characteristically Scottish open crown spire once adorned the tower. There is a fine mural monument of the Renaissance period.

St John's, Perth, is also a fine fifteenth-century church with a remarkable steeple and was the scene of John Knox's denuncia-tion of idolatry in the Church.

Another notable Scottish feature of many of these late Gothic churches is the 'sacrament house', a niche for the consecrated bread, usually elaborately carved. An outstanding group may be seen in the north-east at Kintore, Kinkell, Auchindoir and Deskford (all Grampian). St Mary's, Grandtully (Tayside), is a sixteenth-century work with a timber ceiling on which have been painted various symbolic and armorial subjects.

One of the few medieval remains in modern Dundee is the fifteenth-century steeple of St Mary, the largest and most impressive of its type. Leith has a restored fifteenth-century church of St Mary. St Mary's, Whitekirk (Lothian) is a charming country parish church, largely fifteenth-century, with a two-storeyed medieval tithe barn near by; there is another two-storeyed tithe barn at Foulden (Borders) with corbie gables and outside stair.

Great churches of the fifteenth century are Glasgow Cathedral, Dunkeld Cathedral (Tayside), and outstandingly, St Giles', Edinburgh, and St Machar's, Aberdeen.

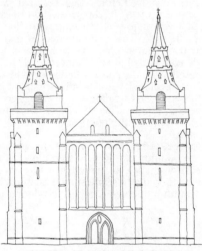

ABERDEEN, ST MACHAR'S CATHEDRAL

Old St Giles' was burnt by Richard II of England in 1385 but by the middle of the fifteenth century, when it was made collegiate by James III, it had not only been rebuilt but considerably enlarged by the addition of numerous chapels and aisles, though the choir was still longer than the nave. The plan which resulted has great breadth and is a very complex version of the late Gothic rectangle. At one time the building was divided internally into four churches and some of the appended parts were put to various secular uses and 'krames' or wooden booths stood against its walls in the French manner.

It has the high broad blunt nave arcade and lofty aisles of the late Gothic period. Apart from some flamboyant window tracery and stumpy pinnacles its most striking exterior feature is the open spire in which flying buttresses, rising from a pierced parapet, support an imperial crown and a diminutive spire. Originally of the fifteenth century, it was restored two hundred years later. In the early nineteenth century William Burn cruelly 'restored' the old fabric, refacing it with paving stones with non-structural joints.

St Machar's, Aberdeen, is the only cathedral built of granite. As is often the case, the nave has been preserved for worship in an otherwise mutilated church; the transepts and east end are gone. But the great architectural triumph is the conception of the west front, a massive heroic design that matches the material in which it is executed. It comprises two spire-capped and machicolated western towers (variations of the broach spire) flanking a gable wall. This is dominated by a round doorway divided into two pointed openings with a vesica between and eight tall slender round-arched 'lancets'; all of this forms a poignant contrast with the sturdy plainness of the towers. Below their plain machicolated parapets the strength, bulky proportions and sparseness and smallness of openings give the design a decidedly martial aspect. The interior is noted for its heraldic ceiling and the tomb of the poet Gavin Douglas, translator of Virgil's *Aeneid*.

King's College, Aberdeen, has a seventeenth-century open spire, with the addition of a Renaissance crown, and preserves a sixteenth-century chapel, a particularly fine specimen of the period, complete with those most rare features to survive in Scotland, beautifully carved screens, rood-loft, and stalls.

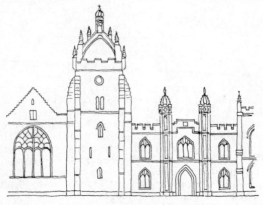

ABERDEEN, KINGS COLLEGE

Another fine work of the fifteenth century is the chapel of the University of St Andrews (old St Salvator's), with its tall tower and octagonal broach spire, and the oldest sacrament house in Scotland. The interior of this and the sixteenth-century chapel of St Leonard are both of much interest.

In the middle ages most larger burghs had many chapels but hardly any survive. One of the few is Magdalene Chapel of the old burgh of Canongate (Edinburgh), once the guild chapel, with almshouses, of the Hammermen. It has the only fragments of stained glass left in Scotland — four armorial roundels — but its little steeple is early seventeenth-century.

The only Scottish monastic house of the Order of Hospitallers or Knights of St John is Torphichen Priory (Lothian), a commandery or cell of their chief English house at Clerkenwell. Though dating from the thirteenth century and much rebuilt, its saddle-roofed transepts and plain central tower are good examples of fifteenth-century church architecture in a military manner, obviously designed for practical use in troubled times. They have upper storeys over the groined vaulting, reached by a spiral stair, and these are furnished with fireplaces and chimneys. The tracery in the transept windows is geometrical but the gables are crow-stepped and of a later date. Altogether it is an interesting amalgam of church architecture with military and domestic elements.

Crossraguel Abbey (Strathclyde) was a Cluniac house that in its fifteenth-century rebuilding was also given a fortified aspect. The aisleless nave without transepts represents the late Gothic tendency towards simplifying the ground plan, and the choir has a three-sided apse showing again the French sympathies of the time. The square tower of the outer court, vaulted over a barn, has rooms above reached by a stair and is equipped with fireplaces and mural closet like a sixteenth-century tower house; it may well have been the abbot's lodging. Also in the outer court is a gatehouse tower — with a stair to its flat roof — of the same date. Worthy of special note are the fifteenth-century rib-vaulted and richly decorated chapter house and sacristy.

The mother house of Crossraguel was Paisley Abbey (Strathclyde), founded in the twelfth century by the Steward of Scotland. But apart from thirteenth-century portions of the south aisle and west front, with their doorways, the present structure is fifteenth-century. The aisled nave is complete and shows a return to an equal division of the interior between main arcade, triforium and clerestory. The arcade is more graceful than is usual in the late Gothic period, whilst the triforium consists of segmented arches springing from dwarf clustered piers. The original feature is the corbelling out over the nave of the triforium passage round the piers, so as not to impair their

PAISLEY ABBEY, DECORATED WINDOW

PAISLEY ABBEY, NAVE

IONA ABBEY,
WINDOW c. 1500

capacity to take the thrust of a high vault. The clerestory reverts to simple tracery in the windows. The very long choir has a fine four-bench sedilia, and the chapel of St Mirren, to whom the church is dedicated, of about 1500, projects from the south transept.

On the north side are a two-storeyed porch and a transept with a large traceried window and buttresses, crowned, as at Dunkeld Cathedral, with corbelled turret-like terminations, another link with the castellated architecture of the period. The tower is finished with a fine pierced parapet, and part of the reconstructed cloister arcade may be seen. Some of the eastern range is incorporated in the nearby seventeenth-century palace.

The chapter house at Glenluce (Dumfries and Galloway) is complete with ribbed vault. Square in plan, it has a tiled floor and traceried windows that resemble those in the chapter house at Crossraguel. The church is thirteenth-century and the water supply system complete with jointed pipes and inspection chambers recalls that in medieval times the monasteries were well above the general level in their provision of practical amenities.

St Mary's Abbey, Iona, was begun in the twelfth century but most of the church belongs to the late fifteenth and early sixteenth centuries, when it became a cathedral church, and it has subsequently been well restored. But because of its distance from the mainstream of architectural activity, its strong Irish affinities and its conservative use of old forms and details it seems much older than that. A cruciform church with a sacristy and south choir aisle, it has a central tower which contained a columbarium or dovecot. There is a chapter house with a scriptorium over and a refectory. The irregular red granite masonry of the abbey is in perfect harmony with its physical setting and at the same time very expressive of its rugged integrity and the persistence of Christian ideals in this exposed and remote place.

Of the same period is the remarkable Ladykirk on the Tweed (Borders), vaulted throughout in the French manner and perhaps a votive church of James IV.

5. Renaissance, c 1500 to c 1600

Palaces

Between the tower houses of the fifteenth century, at the peak of their military strength and potency, and those of the post-Reformation period there is a gap of about a hundred years. Meanwhile, under James IV and James V, Renaissance ideas were introduced and applied to the design of buildings, especially the royal palaces.

Linlithgow Palace (Lothian) on its beautiful site overlooking a loch, was perhaps the finest secular building in Scotland. Ruinous and gaunt since its burning in 1746, it is still immensely impressive. By the fifteenth century it had grown by addition into a quadrangular group, but the elements were not united into a single great structure, largely symmetrical in plan and elevation, until the reconstruction about 1500 by James IV.

LINLITHGOW PALACE

Towers rise from each of the four corners, and staircase towers, slotted with windows, from the angles of the great close or courtyard. An attractive and much ornamented fountain was introduced about 1538, with water piped in through clay and leaden pipes in the manner of a monastic laver. Crow-stepped gables and parapets finished off the upper parts of the palace buildings.

The porch and south entrance now used are James V's alterations, when the architect was James Hamilton. Formerly the entrance was on the east side, guarded by a forework or barbican. It is still remarkable for its elaborate embellishment of niches and sculpture, notably the royal arms over the gateway.

In this wing on the first floor is the Lion Chamber or great

STIRLING
GATEHOUSE

hall, which must have been one of the most splendid rooms in Scotland. It is 100 feet (30 m) long, over 30 feet (9 m) high, and immensely dignified. There is a good moulded doorway, a fine triple fireplace occupying the whole of one end, a buffet cupboard, service hatches, and a mural gallery at the level of the clerestory. It had a stone screen and an open timber roof, except over the dais, where it was barrel-vaulted. At the north end is access to the court kitchen with kitchens and cellarage underneath; at the south end is access to the chapel.

The courtyard has a fine Gothic elevation with sculptured enrichment above the archway dating from about 1530. (The decoration here and on the east facade was once brightly painted.) This is the south facade, which is English in feeling. The wing behind it contains the chapel with fine tall narrow round-headed lancet windows running up through two storeys. It was once paved with tiles, some bearing the love knot cipher of James IV and his queen, Margaret Tudor, the thistle and the rose. There are other apartments here and in the west wing, where the queen's private oratory was, with its oriel window.

The north wing was rebuilt in a neo-classical style in Charles I's time and has an interesting plan and details, such as window pediments; but despite these classical features and an urge towards greater symmetry and balance in the plan the general effect is still late Gothic with a mixture of Renaissance detail and this impression is increased by the close proximity of the palace to the great fifteenth-century town church, itself a splendid example of the period.

The same mixture can be seen at Stirling Castle. The earliest parts are the fifteenth-century gatehouse and the great hall, by Thomas Cochrane, architect to James III, where the window tracery shows Renaissance influence. The hall occupies the east side of the quadrangle. On the south side, connected to the hall at its dais end, is the palace block (1540) of James V, a Gothic building, with crow-stepped gables and parapet, to which large windows (with iron grilles) and Renaissance enrichment have been added, notably in the sculptured heads, putti and full-size figures which stand between the windows on wall shafts, under cusped round arches. Another side is occupied by the Chapel Royal from the last years of the sixteenth century; it has a striking Renaissance facade with classical entrance. Unfortunately, subsequent alterations at Stirling have obscured some of the earlier designs.

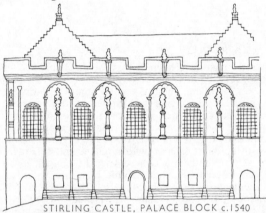
STIRLING CASTLE, PALACE BLOCK c.1540

Although Edinburgh Castle stands on an ancient site most of the buildings, which range round three sides of a courtyard (the fourth being the Scottish National War Memorial), are more recent. On the south side it has the early sixteenth-century Great Hall (old Parliament Hall) with hammer-beam roof and corbels, and on the east, the King's Lodging, remodelled in 1617, with its painted decoration, all that remains of a once sumptuous interior. Also from the sixteenth century is the Half-Moon Battery, which covers the east curtain of the fourteenth-century enceinte with its two towers, one of them the famous tower house of David II. The walls are mostly of the seventeenth and eighteenth centuries and there are military quarters of the early eighteenth century on the west side.

The last of the oblong tower houses were those built about 1500 by James IV at Holyrood and Falkland (Fife), with their oversailing parapets, corner roundels extending from the ground upwards and wide-mouthed gun loops. At Falkland is the late Gothic range to which a Renaissance facade was added. This design, which is a screen in front of the south range of the courtyard, built 1537-42, is most completely in the spirit of the early Renaissance and can claim to be the first facade in that manner in Britain. It has large mullioned windows, wall shafts and portrait medallions, but it is mainly in the proportions and feeling that the Renaissance spirit resides. The stair, too, has a new breadth and ease that is Renaissance rather than Gothic in its affinities and the outstanding features of the outer elevation of the building are the sculptured figures supported on large buttresses. There is a sixteenth-century 'pleasance' garden.

The arrangement of buildings round a courtyard with the hall and kitchen on another side from the lodgings was an English Elizabethan practice and the most 'Elizabethan' building in Scotland is the splendid Palace at Kirkwall (Orkney), built in the early sixteenth century round three sides of a long oblong courtyard. The square-angle towers, however, project in the medieval manner and wide-mouthed gun ports suggest that defensive needs have not been completely overlooked. Both planning and detailing show imagination and sensibility. The hall is a magnificent room on the first floor reached by a new type of staircase that came in with the early Renaissance — the 'scale and platt', with straight flights and landings. From now on there is to be observed a greater appreciation of the spatial possibilities of the stair and its use as an impressive interior feature in its own right. The bay windows and great oriels of the main apartments are skilfully designed and placed.

Perhaps the most attractive addition of the early Renaissance to a medieval castle is the new lodging of the Earl of Nithsdale at Caerlaverock (Dumfries and Galloway) added to the east side of the enceinte, opposite the lodgings. This is a three-storey building of 1634. The facade has steeply pedimented doorways and windows and is enriched with both Gothic heraldry and classical legends, probably the choice of its learned patron. This is a very self-consciously classical building, though compared with the refined neo-classicism of later Palladianism or contemporary work by Inigo Jones it has a quaint and archaic look.

Later tower houses

During the hundred years that led up to the Reformation (1560) there was little need or desire for further tower houses and few were built in that time. Earlshall (Fife) was an exception and its history illustrates very clearly the principle of enlarging tower houses by the addition of further jams or towers. It began as a single tower, to which another square tower was added making an L-plan. An oval tower was then built on to the opposite corner, making a new Z-plan, after which the main building was lengthened.

The Z-plan was particularly preferred in the north-east, where most of the sixty tower houses of this plan are to be found and where it may have originated in the mid-fifteenth century. Each jam commands two sides of the main tower and is in its turn covered, thus providing a tight overlapping system of defence difficult to penetrate. In addition, the desire for more space was also gratified and lighting was improved, for the diagonal position of the jams, round or square, took less light than when set at angles in the L-plan.

Two early Z-plans from about 1570 are Elcho and Castle Menzies, both in Tayside. Though atypical in its planning, the former shows the practice, carried to a high degree, of enlarging a structure by the unit by unit addition of towers, both round and square. The vaulted ground floor contains the kitchen. A stair of increased width leads to the great hall, behind which are two private rooms and from which three stairs lead to separate groups of upper rooms. Interesting features of this picturesque composition are its watch rooms with fireplaces on the roof, its iron yett to the entrance porch, its window gratings and its gun ports, some still with their wooden sills.

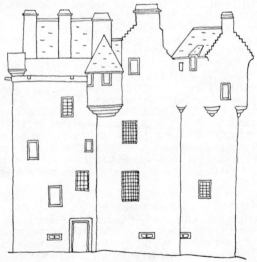

ELCHO CASTLE

Castle Menzies has huge jams and dormers with pediments, round and triangular, and side shafts. Its aesthetic qualities are high with an admirable balance of contrast between the elaboration of the upper parts and the simple severity of the walls. Scale, proportion and the disposition of features and detailing were all well understood by its designer and the less successful nineteenth-century addition underlines this.

One of the most famous of Z-plan towers is Claypotts (Tayside), built 1569-88. Unchanged and complete, it has at the corners two round towers (square within) corbelled out in the upper parts to carry square heads — a lateral expansion of accommodation at a safe height above ground or for decorative effect. The practice became a popular one which was to lead to the development of most elaborate and romantic groupings of the upper features of tower houses in the post-Reformation period. There is continuous provision of wide-mouthed gun ports at ground level. The defensive potentialities of the plan are not in doubt here, and there is a marked shift in the area of interest from the traditional wall-head position. More usually gun loops are rather fortuitously placed, as though they were more for effects of intimidation and ornament — status symbols perhaps — rather than for practical purposes.

Another Z-plan variation of the same date occurs at Glenbuchat (Grampian), which has rectangular towers added. One of these has the main doorway and stair to the first floor, access above being by two spiral staircases at the junction of the jams with the main tower. The stair turrets are borne on squinch arches or trompes in the French manner instead of being corbelled out as was more usual.

The tower house of Amisfield (Dumfries and Galloway) is very high and has a less rustic appearance than Claypotts. Architecturally it is much more sophisticated, despite its simple square plan. It dates from the early seventeenth century and is in five storeys. At the top, great daring is shown in the overhanging and balancing masonry to produce a picturesque group of gables, dormers, chimney stacks and a variety of turrets not so much projecting as suspended at various levels of the elevation. This may be seventeenth-century work but Renaissance influences have clearly scarcely affected the tower-house tradition. The construction of Amisfield is of grey boulders filled with random rubble with dressings of red sandstone. It exemplifies, with the design, the instinctive grasp which the master masons of these towers had for the traditional materials and forms with which they worked: always a sense of fitness yet not incapable of imaginative flights.

On Westray in the Orkneys is the massive mid sixteenth-century Noltland Castle. This is a Z-plan type which shows a

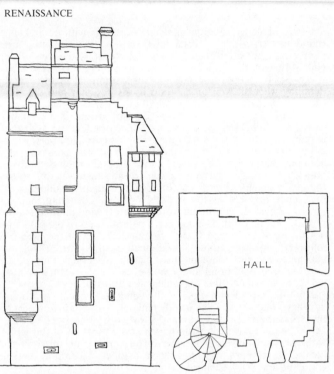

AMISFIELD TOWER   AMISFIELD TOWER

later tendency to lengthen the main building, from which two square towers are offset. It is equipped with some eighty wide-mouthed gun ports arranged in tiers, an astonishingly liberal provision unmatched elsewhere, and its wheel stair shows the new width and easier rise.

Muness (Shetland), a long Z-plan with round towers, has a scale and platt stair of even more advanced design. Yet the earlier L-plan continued to be built, as the late sixteenth-century Castle of Park (Dumfries and Galloway) shows. Tall and imposing, though with only one turret, it nevertheless shows certain features of this later period. The jam has its own gables separate from the main roof and contains the stair up to the third floor, whence a turret stair leads to the roof. A passage or vestibule appears, first on the ground floor — upper rooms are still entered from one another — and large windows give more light to the great hall.

6. Seventeenth-century baronial

Castles and greater houses

From about 1600 there begins the era of the castellated mansion, no more seriously concerned with defence, but very much preoccupied with family pride and social prestige. The Scottish baronial style, the name it acquired retrospectively from the standpoint of Victorian revivalism, reached its apotheosis in the castles of Fraser, Fyvie, Midmar, Tolquhon, Craigievar and Crathes (all in Grampian) and Glamis (Tayside).

At Crathes, the earliest of its group (noted for its remarkable early painted ceilings), the main mass is picturesquely but a little clumsily composed, with a further development in waywardness at the top of the house where the main gables are finished with a straight screen hung between the chimney stacks. A similar example occurs at Glamis, where there are many illogicalities of this kind. They are not always successful but at their best can provide dramatic and interesting effects. The core of Glamis is a fourteenth-century L-plan tower with four storeys with mural chambers. About 1600 a large wing with a round-angle turret was added to the south-east corner and in the seventeenth century a corresponding wing was added to the north-west corner, thus producing a rather elaborate Z-plan. To add to the complexity, in the same century a two storey superstructure was raised above the main block and the whole adorned with clusters of bartizans with steep conical roofs, dormers, chimney stacks and a variety of other features in a composition of exuberant richness.

The plans of these houses are not unusual, nor are the elevations. Their unconventionality lies in the extent to which the romanticism and ostentation of the upper works is carried. While reminiscent of the chateaux of the Loire, this is a specifically Scottish development of native forms. There is an odd variety of design and asymmetry of composition unparalleled in France.

The most splendid of these Scottish baronial houses is perhaps Craigievar (Grampian), an example of the stepped L-plan type, unaltered since it was completed about 1626. Well proportioned and slender, lacking any feeling of ponderous mass, its harled elevations achieve an effect of extraordinary beauty and serenity quite different from the frowning severity of the old 'house of fence'. The varying profile is managed with extraordinary skill and the use of detail and effects of light and shade are exploited with great sensibility.

A typical feature is the mannerism of continuous corbelling below the upper storeys. Now it is staggered in a way that shows it has taken on a purely ornamental role, and it parallels the use of 'false machicolations'. It is a mannerism that appears to go back to the tower of Holyroodhouse (about 1500). Another feature is the use of gun-barrel rainwater spouts at the same level.

Inside, the great hall, with traditional screen, is a striking apartment, its groined vault plastered over and moulded into panels, pendants and a variety of motifs that include classical portrait medallions and heraldic devices. The fireplace too has a huge heraldic panel over it and shows the prominence that such features were given at this time, like the panels over the entrance to ruined Tolquhon Castle (Grampian), a castle of the courtyard type with Z-plan projections of round and square towers, which has triplet pistol holes in the round projecting flanking towers of the 'gatehouse'.

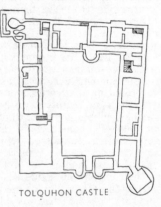

TOLQUHON CASTLE

Tolquhon also illustrates the planning trends of the late sixteenth century in larger establishments, for an oblong fifteenth-century tower house has become a large quadrangular mansion, with forecourt and pleasance.

The elevations of Holyroodhouse (Edinburgh) and Fyvie (Grampian), intended as part of quadrangular schemes, were lengthened by adding a range with a classical front to the tower house and having another built at the other end to balance it. The resultant symmetrical arrangement is a French scheme deriving from the Château d'Ancy-le-Franc (1546) by Sebastiano Serlio, who worked at Fontainebleau, but the translation of the basic forms of the building into the native idiom is far removed from the original source of inspiration. Fyvie is also noted for its imposing but graceful 'wheel' staircase of early Renaissance proportions.

FYVIE CASTLE

The first fully Renaissance building in Scotland, Heriot's Hospital (now School), Edinburgh, was begun in 1627 and paid for out of the fortune of George Heriot, an Edinburgh man who became a London goldsmith banker. He represents a new sort of patron and the designer of Heriot's appears as a new sort of architect whose status ensures that his name, William Wallace, is one of the first to be recorded.

The basic plan of the building, rising above a balustraded terrace, is quadrangular with four square towers at the corners and four stair towers in the courtyard angles. It has many towers and turrets with cupolas, tall chimneys and steeply pedimented windows. In the centre of the main front is a tower carrying a domed and lanterned octagon. The large corner towers with their turrets obviously owe much to the tower-house tradition but the various motifs are rather eclectic including French, Flemish and English ideas. The Renaissance elements here are not just ornamental additions but extend to the overall concep-

GEORGE HERIOT'S HOSPITAL

67

tion of the design. It was Wallace more than anyone who sufficiently cleared the ground of the long-persisting Gothic tradition for Italianate classicism to take root when it was introduced by William Bruce in the last decades of the century.

Similar work of the period can be seen at Linlithgow Palace (north range) and the exterior of the King's Lodging, Edinburgh Castle.

Winton House (Lothian) is another outstanding early Renaissance building by Wallace, dating from 1627, with typical classical ornament and other enrichment: carved pediments, strapwork motifs and twisted stone chimneys of rather English appearance, unlike the corbie gables and irregularly disposed towers and roofs, which are native. King Charles's Room and the drawing room at Winton, with fine carved fireplaces and bold Carolean ceilings, resemble those of Pinkie House (Loretto School), Musselburgh (Lothian), dating some ten years earlier.

Kinneil House (Lothian) is a rather severe combination of seventeenth-century vernacular and the early Renaissance style of Heriot's Hospital. The earlier part of the house has yielded a rare sixteenth-century wall painting depicting the parable of the Good Samaritan, probably of Flemish or French provenance.

Bonhard House (Lothian) is interesting in the way it shows how an earlier house could have its interior refurbished in the style of the seventeenth century. In type it is a simple L-plan with semi-octagonal staircase tower in the re-entrant. The first floor is divided into three remarkable rooms, with panelled walls and moulded plaster ceilings, handsome fireplaces with imposing overmantels panelled for paintings and other features of the period.

Though its castellated exterior is an inspiration of the early nineteenth-century 'Gothick' spirit, The Binns, also in Lothian, is essentially a house of the seventeenth century, an enlargement of an older one, noted for its magnificent Carolean plaster ceilings and friezes of burgeoning fruit and flowers.

A fine example of a nobleman's town mansion of about 1630 is Argyll Lodging, Stirling, which has a courtyard of which buildings form three sides and the fourth is a 6 foot (1.8 m) thick high wall (carrying a passage), with an impressive rusticated gateway with adjacent postern. Opposite the gateway is a richly designed pilastered entrance porch with fluted pilasters carrying an entablature and pediment with an armorial panel above, both decorated with strapwork. The courtyard window decorations are very varied, based on the pediment theme but more like cresting, executed — like the gateway — with barbaric energy; and the dormers are flanked by fluted pilasters like the porch.

The entrance porch leads into a large hall lit from both sides, for the ranges at this time are usually only one room wide. The

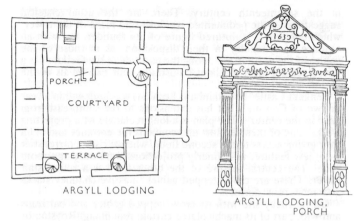

ARGYLL LODGING

ARGYLL LODGING,
PORCH

rooms are still thoroughfare rooms, but a new feature that is found for the first time in larger houses of the period is the large reception room or ballroom. In one vaulted wing are the kitchen and service rooms, in the other the family apartments.

Another fine work of the 1630s is Cowane's Hospital, Stirling, built of attractive white stone, small and well preserved. It was intended to house a dozen needy members of the guild of Stirling and was paid for by a merchant. It is now the Guildhall.

The plan is E-shaped with two projecting wings and a tower in the centre of the front serving as entrance and stair tower. It has its original ogee roof — a new shape which makes its appearance

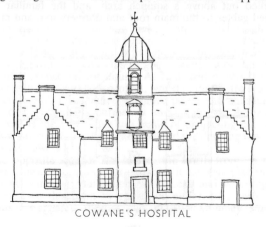

COWANE'S HOSPITAL

balustrade connects them across the centre. The state rooms in the south wing are on the first floor, as is usual with Renaissance houses, but they are still entered from one another as thoroughfare rooms.

The magnificent pile of Drumlanrig Castle (Dumfries and Galloway) though also built in the last quarter of the seventeenth century, is much larger and harks back to Heriot's Hospital. Again the design is quadrangular, arranged round the courtyard.

The main front rises above a terrace over a loggia of round arches carried on square pilastered piers. In the centre of the loggia is a grand double staircase ascending to the main entrance in the large square tower porch, owing something to Heriot's. It finishes with an octagonal stage topped with cupola rising from within a stone ducal coronet.

From each side of this principal front project great square towers, stepped down towards the centre as at Holyroodhouse. These are obviously Scottish 'tower houses' but the facade between is clearly classical with its giant Corinthian pilasters and pedimental windows, albeit steep ones, enriched with carving. The scheme appears to be an attempt to combine two opposing systems appropriate to a Gothic castle and an Italianate house.

Despite the horizontal lines of the balustrades along the terrace and wall-head, and of the cornice (other elevations have traditional corbelling), the chief impression is not of classical horizontality and repose but of a crowded, thrusting roof line. There are roundels on the tower houses and, rising behind these, massive round stair towers in the re-entrants of the courtyard — all with ogee cupola roofs — and many tall chimney stacks. The interior has a great deal of handsome woodwork of the period, oak-panelled with Grinling Gibbons carving.

The main block of Traquair House (Borders) is tall, with high roof, small reticent window openings and dormers; it was built in 1642 and the rambling wings were added later in the same century, but it has a long history going back to the early middle ages. It is a shapely house full of native character, one of the most romantic and picturesque mansions of south Scotland.

At Lennoxlove (Lothian) a commodious seventeenth-century house was added in stages to the old fourteenth-century Lethington Tower, whose rugged barrel-vaulted great hall boldly contrasts with the other rooms of the house, elegantly furnished in the styles of the seventeenth and eighteenth centuries. Characteristically, the first extension in 1626 saw a widening of the stair and enlargement of the windows in the old tower, as a Latin inscription over the entrance records. A tower, replacing a crow-stepped gable, and an upper storey were added in the early nineteenth century.

7. Burgh architecture, c 1600 to c 1800

The crofter's cottage is perhaps the most timeless Scottish vernacular building, preserving until the end of the nineteenth century the type occupied by the Scots peasant farmer. Usually it was a one-storey dry-stone (rubble) or turf-walled structure of turf or thatch weighted with stones suspended from a rope network. Windows were small and few, since glass was a luxury, and a louvre in the roof often had to serve as the only chimney for the central stone hearth. There can have been very little difference between this and a superior iron age dwelling in terms of domestic comfort and convenience, though many people must have been worse off. The 'black house' — as at Shawbost (Lewis, Western Isles) — is the most primitive type, lacking even windows; the more developed 'long house', is extended to provide a byre for cattle under the same roof and the passage between formed a common entrance. Examples can be seen, essentially unchanged, at Valtos (Lewis, Western Isles) and Skerray (Highland) and in Jean Macalpine's inn, Aberfoyle (Central). The most typical example of vernacular architecture of the little and middling sort are found in the many ancient burghs of Scotland, most commonly dating from the sixteenth to the nineteenth century, after which they become, as elsewhere in Britain, standardised housing of no particular character.

The history of most burghs goes back to the first half of the twelfth century, when David I initiated a system of burghs over the whole country as part of the process of turning Scotland into a feudal state on Anglo-Norman lines; among them, timber-built at first, are Edinburgh, Stirling, Perth and Dunfermline.

Though their physical presence has largely vanished, except perhaps for the old kirk or part of a castle, a medieval street plan may be preserved and the layout of market, gates or streets, ports, closes, wynds and vennels may be traced through modern building lines. Examples of old bridges are the narrow thirteenth-century Auld Brig at Ayr (Strathclyde), the fine late medieval Old Stirling (Central) and Haddington (Lothian) bridges and sixteenth-century bridges at Musselburgh (Lothian) and Jedburgh (Borders).

The important economic function of the burgh is expressed by the tolbooth or town house, of which many fine early examples are still in existence, often containing a clock or a peal of bells. Canongate (Edinburgh, 1591), Tain (Highland), Culross (Fife), Stonehaven (Grampian) and the turreted steeple at Glasgow, now deprived of its building, are good examples of this early municipal architecture. Edinburgh's (with a forestair and corbelled turrets) has a hall serving the double purpose of council room timbered facade with Latin inscriptions. Begun in 1570, it allows the three distinct changes which have marked the evolution of the house to be traced and is representative of the lower type of dwelling built on the old garden plots of the city. Later, texts on house fronts were not uncommon.

Early seventeenth-century houses include Gladstone's Land, Lady Stair's House, Moray House and Acheson House. Gladstone's Land — the word was apparently given to buildings where each floor was separately let — is a tall dignified six-storeyed burgess's house with crow-stepped gables and outside stair, an old double arcade on the ground floor and interesting interior with seventeenth-century painted timber ceilings. The last two features are both early Renaissance features, as are the fine plaster ceilings at Moray House with its corbelled balcony and pyramidal gateway.

Gladstone's Land is the last of the old High Street facades which at one time were six or seven storeys high. Squeezed within the safe circuit of its wall, the city grew upwards in the French fashion, its citizens in their flats and tenements thoroughly urbanised in their quite un-English way and showing, in another context from the fortified tower house, the national propensity for high building.

Acheson House (1633) is an interesting example of the town house of the courtyard type like the magnificent Argyll Lodging, Stirling; while Hamilton House, Prestonpans (Lothian), though of the same period and built for an Edinburgh burgess, preserves the old L-plan. It has a polygonal porch in the re-entrant, dormers, large chimney stacks and corbie gables. Near the old harbour of Leith is a combined merchant's dwelling and warehouse of four storeys known as Lamb's House, dating from the sixteenth century. With its tall facade, high roof, irregularly disposed shuttered windows and projecting stair tower it has something of the stern defensive mien of the old tower house about it, notwithstanding its crow-stepped gables.

In Ayr (Strathclyde), Loudon Hall overlooking the harbour was built by a local burgess in the sixteenth century, whilst in Aberdeen the oldest surviving house is Provost Ross's from the last years of the same century. Provost Skene's House, on the other hand, is a good piece of turreted domestic vernacular of the seventeenth century. Lanark (Strathclyde), in Hyndford House, has a good specimen of a nobleman's town house and Jedburgh (Borders) has Queen Mary's House with turrets and corbie gables.

Culross (Fife) is the most interesting and picturesque of a number of very interesting burghs in the ancient Kingdom of Fife, some of which possess typical smaller parish kirks such as St Monans, St Dronstan's, Markinch, and Crail whilst the six-

teenth-century towers of Holy Trinity, St Andrews, and Pittenweem are towers of the 'Fife' type with a strong castle-like air
about them. Cupar has a fifteenth-century tower and seventeenth-century spire.

Of post-Reformation churches, the Tron Church, Edinburgh
(really Christ's Church but named after the nearby public weigh
beam), is a mutilated remnant dating from 1637. The spire is an
unfortunate nineteenth-century replacement of John Mylne's
original. The Tron Steeple at Glasgow is all that remains of the
1637 church of St Mary's. At Largs (Strathclyde) the Skelmorlie
Aisle of the Old Kirk dates from 1636 and has a painted timber
roof and tombs of the founder and his wife. The Old Kirk at Ayr
was built in 1654 from funds provided by Oliver Cromwell when
he requisitioned the site of an earlier thirteenth-century church
of St John (the tower still stands) in order to build his citadel
there. More often than with medieval churches, ruined by
Knox's 'rascal multitude', these post-Reformation churches have
interesting interior fittings and at Ayr there are separate 'lofts'
for sailors, traders and merchants. Cullen Collegiate Church
(Grampian) of the sixteenth century (with sacrament house and
good tombs) has the Seafield 'gallery', a fine seventeenth-
century laird's pew; but perhaps the finest is in the church at
Abercorn (Lothian), where above a vault is a gallery embellished with carving, off which open pine-panelled retiring rooms
from which a 'squint' gives a view of the minister. It was
designed by Sir William Bruce, for the Hopes of nearby
Hopetoun. Otherwise it has a bare and dignified simplicity.

Post-Reformation churches tended to shun the more obviously
Gothic forms and features and nowhere is this more clearly
shown than in the group of Caithness (Highland) churches
among which are Dunnet, Reay and Canisbay. Extremely simple
in form, harled and whitewashed, they have a Scandinavian aura
about them that fits well with the new faith. Burntisland (Fife)

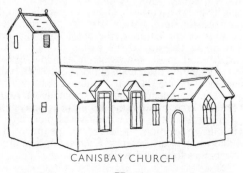

CANISBAY CHURCH

was perhaps modelled on a Dutch church and has a sailors' loft and outside stair like the tower at Reay. Here in the earliest surviving post-Reformation church in Scotland, with its octagonal bell-tower, the Presbyterian practice of making the pulpit the focus of the church can be clearly seen in a singularly chaste interior.

The parish church at Cromarty (Highland) is severely plain but carefully preserves in its interior much original woodwork of an archaic kind, including lofts (an ornate one for the laird, a simpler one for the poor) supported on square posts and exposed joists. The parish church of Glenbuchat (Grampian) was reconstructed in the eighteenth century. Typical of its kind, the plain interior is arranged with pews — with cobbles between — on three sides of the pulpit in the south wall, where the doors and most windows are. There is a laird's loft and other box pews. Canongate Church (1688), Edinburgh, has a plain spacious interior, an apse and a portico. By the eighteenth century churches began to assume a classical garb, if often modified by more homespun native qualities, and examples of these may be seen at Gifford (Lothian), Newton Mearns (Strathclyde), Ceres (Fife), Killin (Central), Inveraray (Strathclyde), St Nicholas, Lanark (Strathclyde) and the octagonal parish church at Kelso (Borders). Nevertheless, throughout this period there were many country parishes with no more than a small primitive barn-like kirk with a thatched or turfed roof and pews only for a few elders or the laird's family.

Culross (Fife) have has a good quota of other kinds of old buildings: houses of mariners and merchants that are solid stone-built, often harled, with small windows, dormers, 'corbie' Flemish gables, red pantiled roofs, large 'lums' or chimneys and occasionally panelled rooms. There are many forestairs; the interesting old tolbooth has a double one, a typical feature of old towns.

Elie and Earlsferry, Pittenweem and Crail (all in Fife) have similar dwellings with corbie gables and pantiled roofs set in their characteristic steep narrow streets; at Crail these lead, significantly, from the harbour (the oldest unspoilt one on the east coast) up to the site of the castle.

The largest and most impressive house in Culross is the Palace, an outstanding town mansion of about 1600. It displays a strong flavour of native domestic building, seasoned by Dutch and Scandinavian influences and the Italianate or Renaissance features already recognised in the more pretentious palaces and houses. Among the latter are columns and mouldings — if of somewhat odd proportions — arcading, pedimented dormer windows and plasterwork ceilings. Special features are the fine painted timber ceilings and walls.

Many towns prospered and expanded in the eighteenth century and offer many examples of Georgian town houses. Among the most attractive are Haddington (Lothian), Kelso and Selkirk (Borders), Kirkcudbright (Dumfries and Galloway), Elgin (Grampian) and Inverness, Tain and Cromarty in Highland.

Haddington, with one the best High Streets in Scotland, has a good deal of unassertive charm that derives from its characterful native vernacular together with the dignity and grace of its eighteenth-century town houses. Of particular note are Haddington House and Moat House of the seventeenth century and the pleasing and unusual Palladian house where Jane Welsh was born, with its miniature 'palace' front. In Perth (Tayside) Rose Terrace is a good example of the period, while Arbuthnot House, Peterhead (Grampian), dates from the turn of the century.

A different type of eighteenth-century design is the Arched House, Ecclefechan (Dumfries and Galloway), where the writer Thomas Carlyle was born. Built by his father and uncle, both master masons, it shows what a more localised tradition produced. Lockerbie not far away has many attractive houses in a variety of styles and local stones which blend together in a way which illustrates the harmonising power of good vernacular building.

At Kelso (Borders) the square is of great architectural interest. In addition to the Palladian Town House (1816) with Georgian turret and its handsome church, this well-planned dignified burgh has interesting old coaching inns and shops, especially the double row in Bridge Street.

At Selkirk (Borders) the streets radiate from a pleasing central square flanked by a number of handsome houses and at Kirkcudbright (Dumfries and Galloway), well planned with many eighteenth-century houses, Auchengool House and Broughton House are fine examples of the seventeenth and eighteenth centuries respectively, besides the earlier house of Provost Maclellan. Inveresk (Lothian) is a very complete and well preserved village of attractive seventeenth and eighteenth-century vernacular, with two good sixteenth-century houses and a Georgian manor house and church.

Coupar Angus (Tayside) is typical of its region with its square and narrow streets lined with stone houses, rather grave and austere in aspect. Cromarty (Highland) has some fine Georgian architecture in old red sandstone, instead of red brick as was more typical in England. Cromarty House, with main block and two small low wings, is strangely urban so far in the rugged north but the Court House (1782) is of equal interest with its entrance tower, octagon and cupola. There is an eighteenth-century

CROMARTY HOUSE

Gaelic chapel, a manse and an eighteenth-century industrial monument in the old brewery. Because of its economic decline the town has changed little.

A number of towns date in the present form from the last quarter of the eighteenth century and were often the foundation of some nobleman who wished either to tidy up and rehouse a local township adjacent to his seat or to sponsor a new settlement for commercial reasons. Inveraray (Strathclyde) was given its Georgian character by the Duke of Argyll, whose castle towers over it, whereas Portgordon (Grampian), whose original character has now been largely replaced, was founded at the end of the century as a fishing settlement by the Duke of Gordon. Eaglesham and Helensburgh (both in Strathclyde) were both laid out as exercises in eighteenth-century town planning, whilst more remotely at Ullapool (Highland) on Loch Broom a fishing township was built as a station in 1786 by the British Fisheries Society as a traditional industry expanded; it still retains much of its former appearance. Modern Wick (Highland) is the product of a union between the irregularly formed old fishing port and, south of the river, the planned layout of Pulteneytown (1787) by the famous engineer Thomas Telford. The contrast between the two is striking. The modern Highland resort of Grantown-on-Spey (Highland) was founded ten years earlier by Sir James Grant, and Tomintoul (Grampian) is another example of eighteenth-century town design.

In Lothian in particular the agricultural changes following enclosure were responsible for some fine stone farm buildings, often with more than one quadrangular court for winter fattening of cattle. Fine stone dovecots — usually circular in plan and once housing up to a thousand birds each — are a feature of many large country house or ecclesiastical farm sites. They frequently date from the late middle ages or sixteenth century but were in general use at least until the eighteenth century,

27. *Argyll's Lodging, Stirling, Central Region.*

28. *The Wallace Monument, near Stirling, Central Region.*

29. *(Left) The tolbooth, Tain, Highland.*

30. *(Right) The tolbooth, Musselburgh, Lothian.*

31. *(Left) The tolbooth, Crail, Fife.*

32. *(Right) The tolbooth, Sanquhar, Dumfries and Galloway*

33. The townhouse at Haddington, Lothian.

34. The Mercat Cross, Prestonpans, Lothian.

35. John Knox's House in Edinburgh.

36. The 'Little Houses' in the square at Dunkeld, Tayside.

37. Rose Terrace, including Ruskin's House, Perth, Tayside.

38. Broughton House, Kirkcudbright, Dumfries and Galloway.

39. *The dovecot at Aberdour Castle, Fife.*

40. *Robert Burns's Cottage at Alloway, Strathclyde.*

41. *Preston Mill, East Linton, Lothian.*

42. *The school at New Lanark, Strathclyde.*

43. Ruthven Barracks, near Kingussie, Highland.

44. Fort George, Highland.

45. Wade's Bridge, Aberfeldy, Tayside.

46. Kinross House, Tayside.

47. *Blair Castle, Blair Atholl, Tayside.*

48. *Atholl Palace Hotel, Pitlochry, Tayside.*

49. *Cally House Hotel, Gatehouse of Fleet, Dumfries and Galloway.*

50. *Culzean Castle, Strathclyde.*

51. Lochinch Castle, near Stranraer, Dumfries and Galloway.

52. The Forth Road Bridge (suspension bridge) and the rail bridge behind.

53. The theatre at Pitlochry, Tayside.

when agrarian changes made the damage inflicted on crops by so many birds no longer tolerable. A good specimen of the beehive type (there are other types) is the dovecot at East Linton (Lothian) with its strange roof shape. Other examples are to be seen at Corstorphine, Edinburgh, and Tealing (Tayside).

With humbler farmhouses and dwellings, such as the eighteenth-century cottages of Swanston (Lothian), the thatched cottages of Burns at Alloway (Strathclyde) and Hugh Millar's at Cromarty (Highland), with its corbie gables, the old indigenous style had changed little since the later medieval period — notwithstanding the odd classical trimming or windows of Georgian proportions. It persisted into the nineteenth century in the single-storey cottages of farm labourers and colliers built in local stone. As the commonest building material in Scotland, stone is to a large extent responsible for the strong, enduring quality of so much of the architecture and for the harmony between the buildings and the environment. The granite of the north-east has a dour character, though capable of great brilliance; but the red sandstones, old and new, were extensively used and are most attractive, expecially where they outcrop in their native districts.

Among the buildings which belong to the early days of the industrial revolution are Shuttle Row, Blantyre (Strathclyde), with the tenement (1780) which was Livingstone's birthplace, the watermill at Preston Mill (Lothian), the mill at Catrine (Strathclyde), which once had a giant waterwheel, and the handloom weaver's cottage at Kilbarchan (Strathclyde). Robert Owen's textile mills at New Lanark (Strathclyde) had a European reputation in their day as the centre of a socio-industrial experiment; but the later industrial buildings of the Forth-Clyde valley lost most of the massive simplicity and noble proportions of the early engineering architecture and grew from a trickle into a menacing flood. Between 1850 and 1900 the built-up area of Edinburgh doubled in size.

Fortifications of the seventeenth and eighteenth centuries

The seventeenth century saw the end of the military role of the Scottish tower house and the forts which were constructed as a result of the Cromwellian occupation (1651-60) and the pacification of the Highlands following the Jacobite Risings of 1715 and 1745 owed much to continental practice.

Round bastions had given way to angled ones and Sébastien de Vauban, Louis XIV's great engineer, developed the system in which all faces and angles were swept by crossfire and outworks were supported from behind but, once taken, exposed to fire from within.

There are only traces now of Oliver's Fort ('the Sconce') on the right bank of the river Ness at Inverness, but the old clock tower still stands on the site. It appears to have been a large pentagon, surrounded by a wide ditch, with low three-pointed bastions projecting at each angle. 'Streets' of barracks and stables ran parallel to the sides round parade grounds.

A coastal fort of the late seventeenth century is Fort Charlotte, Lerwick (Shetland). Its architect was John Mylne, the king's master mason, and it was erected against the Dutch, who eventually burned it. Restored in the eighteenth century, its plan is pentagonal with bastions projecting from the angles.

There are early eighteenth-century forts at Ruthven near Kingussie (Highland) and Braemar (Grampian). At the first of these, two large barrack blocks of three storeys face one another across a parade ground. They have typically austere versions of a Georgian elevation. The other two sides are walls with gun embrasures whilst at opposite corners of the square two-storey blocks project. Braemar was an old tower house adapted, yet again, to new conditions and needs by throwing round it a star-shaped curtain wall with loops for musketry.

Fort Augustus (Highland), now part of the abbey, was both fort and seat of the Governor and therefore had to be a more complex and imposing design. Pointed bastions project from the angles of its square plan and it was enclosed by ramparts.

The greatest of these Hanoverian fortifications is the second Fort George at Ardersier (Highland), dating from the middle of the eighteenth century and still entire and in use. Here William Skinner engineered a large garrison fortress on a peninsula thrusting out into the Moray Firth. Approaching it by various outworks and a glacis slope, the attacker would reach a ravelin or outwork. From this a timber bridge crosses a wide water ditch to the massive pedimented entrance in the ramparts of the enceinte — huge earthworks faced with stone — from which protrude full bastions, flat bastions and demi-bastions such as were required by the principles of contemporary fortification.

General Wade's road system, designed to open up the wild Highlands and connect the military centres, is well known not only for the contribution it made to the life of the region but also as the real origin of the Ordnance Survey. During the course of its construction many bridges were built, the grandest and most famous of them being the one over the river Tay at Aberfeldy (Tayside). At the other extreme are small rubble-built arched bridges such as that on the 'military road' which runs between Fort Augustus and Laggan. This type is really the 'packhorse' bridge of the seventeenth and eighteenth centuries, of which one of the largest and finest spans Gala Water (Borders).

8. Eighteenth-century classicism, c 1680 to c 1830

Palladian and later Georgian

The next architectural period begins with William Bruce, whose work has already been noticed at Drumlanrig House. Bruce was a contemporary of Christopher Wren and his work belongs to the seventeenth century. But he was also the first exponent of that neo-classic style — distinct from the early Renaissance work of Heriot's — which became the most characteristic manner of important commissions of the eighteenth century.

Bruce's early career is obscure but that he was capable of an essentially Gothic design can be seen from the square tower with four diminishing stages he designed in the 1650s for the Merchants' House, Glasgow. His first design in the neo-classic style was the remodelling and extension of the Palace of Holyroodhouse, Edinburgh, which began in 1671 following his appointment as superintendent of royal buildings. The work was carried out by the chief master mason to the Crown, Robert Mylne. The scheme involved the extension of a tower house of about 1500 by the addition of a range to one side of it, terminating in a duplicate tower, the main entrance being placed in the centre with a royal crown in stone above and flanked with coupled Doric columns. The corner towers have enlarged windows and are stepped down on the inner side in the manner of Drumlanrig. The effect of this is a basically French Renaissance disposition of elements translated into the Scottish idiom.

But behind this entrance facade lie the courtyard elevations with their rows of pilasters in three orders, Doric, Ionic and Corinthian, corresponding to their division into three storeys, and their restrained pedimented windows; and there is also a loggia with round arches carried on square piers. Here for the

PALACE OF HOLYROODHOUSE

first time is the authentic Palladian manner, the form of neo-classicism first introduced by Inigo Jones. This is the first instance of its use and it marks an important innovation in Scottish architecture, pointing forward to Hopetoun and the grand manner of the eighteenth century. The Italianate ceilings of the interior at Holyrood are in the style of the seventeenth century, the dining room is in the later Adam style and the state apartments are Victorian. The entrance gateway is a notable example of its kind.

Another of Bruce's major works which looks forward to a more correct neo-classic form of expression is Kinross House (1785-95) (Tayside), superficially a large compact house in the style of Wren with large roof, tall chimneys and a lantern. A closer look reveals French elements and a certain Scottishness in the way these foreign forms are handled. The rather eccentric way the relationship between the giant order of Corinthian pilasters and the entablature that appears to rest upon them is expressed recalls illogicalities already noted at Drumlanrig, for there is a considerable spacing between the pilasters, giving the impression that the entablature is inadequately supported in the manner called for by the syntax of classical design. An ornamented gate leads into the formal garden which is a feature of the total design.

Bruce built his own house at Balkaskie (Fife), Prestonfield House and also Auchendinny (Lothian), in 1707, the last house he did. Though it is the smallest too, it does show a move away from the compact plan to a more spreading composition for it consists of a main block from which pavilions extend on each side. At Thirlestane Castle (Borders), with its full complement of 'baronial' features, the fine west front is his. There are splendid late Stuart interiors — notably the long drawing room with the fine plaster ceiling, the work of Dutch craftsmen.

Hopetoun House (Lothian), overlooks the Firth of Forth. Bruce's part, owing much to Clarendon House in London, was begun in 1696 and can be seen today as the west side of the centre block on the opposite side from the present main front, though originally it too had a courtyard on the site of the existing one. The facade of the west side of the centre block is a twin-towered design which the large roof dominates in a French manner. This is also the style of the high segmental pediment over the centre, a motif associated elsewhere with Bruce, for example on the porch and windows at Drumlanrig.

This earlier work at Hopetoun was finished in 1703. Eighteen years later an enlargement of the house was begun for the Earl by William Adam senior, Bruce's pupil and clerk of works at Hopetoun. He was an important figure in his own right and, as father of the famous Adam brothers, an essential link in the

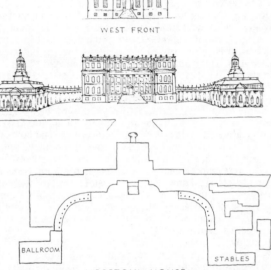

WEST FRONT

HOPETOUN HOUSE

chain of architectural tradition in Scotland. With another patron, Sir John Clerk of Penicuik, Adam made a tour of English country houses in 1727 which was destined to enlarge his ideas and influence the course of country-house building in eighteenth-century Scotland.

A good part of the earlier house at Hopetoun was now demolished, the centre block widened, the present flanking wings and pavilions constructed and the connecting colonnades turned into concave curves in the usual fashion of eighteenth-century houses on this plan. The east facade, therefore, is almost all the design of William Adam. After his death in 1748 his work was carried on by two of his sons, John and Robert, and it was they who remodelled the main entrance and the pavilions to their present form and who were responsible for the decoration of the principal apartments, for which James Cullen provided the furniture.

The panelled dining room, library and state bedroom are Bruce's while the Adams designed the state dining room, the red and yellow drawing rooms, the entrance hall and the ballroom in the south pavilion, opposite the stable wing. The main staircase under the central cupola has bold naturalistic carving in the style of Grinling Gibbons and balusters of the same period.

The east and west facades of Hopetoun exhibit an interesting contrast between the heavier, more compact French classicism of Bruce and the lighter, more expansive Palladian manner of the Adams, with its round-headed windows, triangular pediments, elegant cupolas and lanterns, and balustrades punctuated by classical urns. Here the echoes are not French but English, reminiscent of Gibbs and, in particular, Vanbrugh, the architect of the great palaces of Blenheim and Castle Howard in England.

The setting of Hopetoun in its landscaped garden is typically English, the formal balance and the regularity of the house being agreeably contrasted with the informality of nature in a way which was admired by lovers of the picturesque. The landscaped garden was supposed, under certain conditions, to be reminiscent of the Roman Campagna as seen through the eyes of that much admired painter Claude, a nostalgic romantic conception rather than a classical one. The European fashion for such parks, widely known through the work of Lancelot 'Capability' Brown, spread to Scotland. Even the grounds of an old castellated mansion like Glamis were laid out by Brown in the new taste of the eighteenth century.

Another work of William Adam is Yester House (Lothian), with its fine landscaped park and avenue leading to the village of Gifford, where the church, built 1710, is a good example of the early Georgian period. At Drum (Lothian) and Dumfries House, Cumnock (Strathclyde), his original schemes and his furnishings have been carefully preserved. He was the first Scottish architect to employ Italian craftsmen to cover the ceilings and interior walls with low relief stucco panels instead of the wooden panelling of the seventeenth century. The Drum is an old house recased. Boldly modelled with channelled masonry, it has more of Vanbrugh's heavier, dramatic qualities than the typical Palladian house. Duff House, Banff (Grampian), is a splendid house of about 1735 inspired by the Villa Borghese. Its outward magnificence is matched by fine classic interiors. Marchmount (Borders) and Pollock, in Glasgow, are two more examples.

Another remarkable design was Chatelherault, Hamilton (Strathclyde), a shooting lodge designed as a grand entrance gate flanked by lodges, intended to close a vista from the former Hamilton Palace, since demolished because of mining subsidence. William Adam also designed the octagonal church (1732) at Hamilton, Blairadam House (Tayside), built for himself, Haddo House (Grampian), the wings at Mellerstain (Borders), and Edinburgh Royal Infirmary.

As master mason of the Ordnance Board, engaged on repairing castles and constructing fortifications after the 'Forty-Five' he was associated particularly with the first Fort George (Highlands), where he was succeeded by his son John.

In 1715 Colin Campbell burst upon the architectural scene with the first volume of his monumental *Vitruvius Britannicus,* a collection of drawings which did even more to establish the Palladian style for country houses than Lord Burlington and the rest of his group. Powerful though their influence was, Campbell's was earlier. Several of the designs were described as being in the manner of Jones and Palladio and among them were some for the Duke of Argyll and Lord Islay. His own edition of Palladio's *Architecture* came out in 1729 but he died in the same year. His chief works in England belong to the 1720s and include Mereworth (a copy of one of Palladio's villas in the Veneto), Stourhead and his masterpiece, Houghton Hall, for the prime minister, Sir Robert Walpole. He also did a number of earlier, less grand houses in Scotland. As an innovator of architectural motifs he is remembered as the first to build a hexastyle portico.

Lord Burlington became Campbell's pupil and whilst Burlington and his protégé, William Kent, were engaged on the inside of Burlington House, Campbell was employed in remodelling the outside with another Scottish architect, James Gibbs, who was later to become his bitter rival.

Born in Aberdeen, Gibbs went to Rome for professional training under the baroque architect Carlo Fontana — an unusual advantage at that time — before returning home to publish two excellent books which did much to disseminate the ideas of Wren, especially in his later baroque manner. His own suitably scholarly work at Oxford and Cambridge sometimes inclines to the baroque and sometimes to the Palladian. The architect of St Martin-in-the-Fields, Gibbs made a great name for himself in London but unfortunately his only well known Scottish work is the design for the West Church of St Nicholas in his native city, completed in 1755. But it is one of the best examples of its kind.

St Andrew's Church, Glasgow, also dates from the middle of the century. By Alan Dreghorn, it is based on the design of Gibbs's St Martin-in-the-Fields except for the spire — a thoroughly unclassical convention. St Andrew's Episcopal Church, Glasgow, is another work of the same period.

Of William Adam's four talented sons, Robert is outstanding. After matriculating at Edinburgh University, he went to Rome in 1754 with Lord John Hope. From there he visited Diocletian's Palace at Spalato (Split) on the Adriatic as he was particularly interested in Roman domestic architecture. His drawings were published in 1764 but six years before that he had begun to practise in London.

His work is characterised by the very personal interpretation of classical themes in which the robust gravity and rigid correctness of Palladianism gave way to a lighter, freer, more romantic style. In this sense it was transitional. He introduced greater movement and variety into his designs, with curving forms and contrasting shapes. As well as the usual Renaissance motifs, Adam used Greek and Pompeian or late Roman ones, adopting a light, delicate style of interior decoration in forms and pale colours. Shallow domes, alcoves, apses and reciprocity of floor and ceiling designs are all elegant characteristic features.

He refined neo-classicism in a way which came to dominate the Georgian architecture of the late eighteenth century as Palladianism had dominated it in the first part. In the process he established a style of design that was to contribute much to the whole range of applied art from Wedgwood pottery to Sheraton furniture. Publication of *The Works in Architecture of Robert and James Adam* in 1773 did much to ensure the spread of their ideas.

MELLERSTAIN HOUSE

At Mellerstain (Borders) the two wings were built by William Adam senior in 1725 but the centre block is the work of Robert, about 1770. Its elegant facades are crenellated concessions to the Scottish tradition of castellated architecture but the effect is restrained and mitigates little of their urbane eighteenth-century look. The library is a most magnificent room and its ceiling and friezes show Adam's decorative genius at its happiest.

Culzean Castle (Strathclyde) dates from a few years later. Here the site is an old one overlooking the sea and the exterior, as at Mellerstain, is crenellated and classically symmetrical. The design, however, is a much more thoroughly 'castellated' one in its massing and detail, and its vertical emphases such as round towers and cross loops. The terrace is crenellated like the roof line. It is a bold eighteenth-century 'Gothick' composition, the first light-hearted revival of medieval building that was to mature into the solemn Gothic revival of the next century. The castellation has none of the features which later became identified with Scottish baronial houses. It is essentially the manner adopted by Robert Smirke when he came to do Eastnor Castle in 1808 and serves to show what an early example of the style Culzean is.

The interior decoration at Culzean is among Adam's best work and of special note are the oval staircase, the round drawing room and the plaster ceilings. The original fittings and furniture demonstrate his astonishingly thorough attention to every detail of a decorative scheme, from ceiling designs and mantelpieces to escutcheons and door knobs. It is in this comprehensiveness that the pervading sense of unity of his best compositions resides.

Robert worked on the interiors at Yester House, after his father, and there the splendid saloon with its Palladian ceiling and subtle yellow walls blends the two manners in a scheme of great magnificence. The monumental gates may also be his.

In 1790 Robert built diminutive Seton Castle (Lothian) to replace the magnificent old palace there. It is castellated Georgian 'Gothick' of the same order as Culzean, and perhaps even more successful. Gosford Park (Lothian) is an Adam design realised in 1870, long after his death, by William Young, the architect of the Municipal Buildings, Glasgow. Lauderdale House, Dunbar (Lothian), now a barracks, is also Robert Adam's work.

Foulis Castle (Highland) is an eighteenth-century mansion with some Dutch features while Leigh Hall (Grampian) is interesting for the way a turreted house of about 1650 has been enlarged in the eighteenth century so as to make the architecture of the two periods into an organic unity. It also shows that the baronial manner was strong enough to persist in a century that was more alien to it in many ways than the nineteenth century, which revived it.

A fine, largely Georgian house and a typical product of the social changes going on around the growing capital is Arniston House (Lothian), where development during the seventeenth and eighteenth centuries kept level with the rising fortunes of the Dundases.

In Edinburgh Robert and John Adam built the Palladian Royal Exchange (1753) (now the City Chambers) with its Corinthian pilasters supporting a pediment; but a more original and sensitive design was that for the General Register House (1772) with its characteristic flat central dome, elegant flanking towers, grand staircase and restrained ornament. It was designed to face the new North Bridge by Mylne and is the Adams' counterpart to Sir William Chambers's Somerset House in London, with which it makes an interesting comparison. The new buildings which Robert added to his old university from

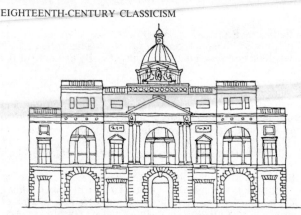

TRADES HOUSE

1789 were later altered. Glasgow still preserves his Trades House (1791), with its magnificent hall, for its original purpose.

It was at Edinburgh that Adam was given his biggest chance to show what he could do in large-scale town design. The original plan for what was styled the New Town, projected by Provost Drummond as part of the city's development programme in the late eighteenth century, was the work of James Craig, who trained under Sir Robert Taylor and won the competition in 1767. Bold and simple, it made an admirable use of the site.

Old Edinburgh was a teeming, congested, socially mixed settlement of narrow wynds and closes, 'lands' and tenements, but with the construction of the North Bridge in 1772 over the Nor' Loch it was now free to expand into an eighteenth-century conception of town planning that makes an astonishing contrast with the medieval and seventeenth-century city. The difference between the Royal Mile (Canongate, High Street and Lawnmarket) and West Bow on the one hand and George Street, with the streets at right angles to it between Princes Street and Queen Street, on the other, is most eloquent. Here in the New Town the tall rational terraces and spacious stately squares are what the late eighteenth century saw as a necessary background for elegant and civilised urban living. Even the gardens, like those at Queen Street, which occupied the centres of the squares were part of the fashionable movement to establish a relationship between picturesque nature and the formal architecture of the town.

Craig designed the Physicians' Hall (1774), later demolished, as well as other buildings which were part of his scheme; but, though modified, it is Adam's contribution to the earlier work which claims the greatest attention. Some of his houses in Castle

EDINBURGH, ROYAL BANK OF SCOTLAND

Street and Queen Street survive and it was he who was responsible for Charlotte Square with its magnificent symmetrical 'palace' facade (about 1790), beautifully proportioned, and the columned and pedimented centre piece linked to pilastered 'pavilions' over a rusticated ground floor. In this are inconspicuously set the doorways of the individual houses. This splendid building occupies the north side of the square. The south side is later, by Sir Robert Reid, and St George's parish church is Playfair's. The Assembly Rooms date from 1787.

St George's was intended to be balanced by another church, St Andrew's, at the other end of George Street. Oval in plan by Major Fraser (its delicate steeple is the work of Sibbald), it was displaced to the north side of George Street by the grand Palladian town house, now the Royal Bank of Scotland, built by Sir William Chambers for Sir Lawrence Dundas. By contrast, Buccleuch Place (1780), to the south of the old town, is an example of simpler residential development providing flats for persons of more modest means.

When the South Bridge was built in 1785 that side of the city was developed and there is still much of the earlier architecture of this phase to be seen, including Adam's work at the University. Other works by him in Edinburgh are the old Observatory and the Roman monument to David Hume in Calton cemetery.

Robert Adam became an FRS but was never a member of the Royal Academy, unlike his principal professional rival in the last part of the eighteenth century, Sir William Chambers. Both shared the distinction of being architect to the Crown.

Chambers was born in Sweden into a Scots merchant family. His prolific work is largely confined to England. His style was a more vigorous, if severer version of Palladianism than Adam's, as can be seen from his scholarly restrained *magnum opus*, Somerset House. It was one of the earliest buildings specifically designed to accommodate the expanding administration of the United Kingdom as well as learned societies.

In Edinburgh he built Duddingston House (1768) and later the town mansion (now the Royal Bank) for Sir Lawrence Dundas in St Andrew Square in the New Town.

Another enterprising Scot abroad was Charles Cameron, architect to Catherine the Great in St Petersburg (now Leningrad). Like Adam's, his work moves from Palladianism to a more romantic classicism.

St Andrew's Square, Glasgow, dates from the mid eighteenth century when the city was expanding its trade in the era of the 'tobacco lords'. With Allan Dreghorn's fine classical church (with its slender Scottish steeple) at its centre, it set the pattern for Glasgow squares centred on major architectural works.

Robert Mylne was both architect and bridge builder. He was the son of a city surveyor of Edinburgh and went to study in Rome. In 1760 he won a competition for Blackfriars Bridge in London, which led to many more important commissions, which are distinguished both for their architectural grace and for their extremely able engineering. Among them were the North Bridge (1772), Edinburgh, reconstructed in 1897, and Jamaica Street Bridge, Glasgow. His best known building in Scotland is St Cecilia's Hall, Edinburgh, a work of the early 1760s based on the Parma opera house, now restored, but without its portico. It is an interesting example of an early concert hall patronised by fashionable Georgian society. His great classical mansion of Cally House in its fine grounds at Gatehouse of Fleet (Dumfries and Galloway) is now a hotel.

He followed Roger Morris at Inveraray (Strathclyde), where the two architects had the assistance of the Adams, first the father and then the son John. The castle there, on a fifteenth-century site, was transformed by about 1780 into a castellated mansion, less 'Gothick' in its exterior than Culzean and more Scottish with its crenellated projection round towers with high conical roofs and its high dormers.

In the town Mylne did the Palladian church — divided for services in English and Gaelic — with its pedimented front and steeple, the impressive Argyll Arms, and perhaps the Town House.

Inveraray was rebuilt from 1743 as a model township, an early example of unified comprehensive planning. Eaglesham (Strathclyde) is another planned village of the late eighteenth century created by a nobleman, with its own church of about 1790.

Fochabers (Grampian) is a most handsome example of late

INVERARAY CASTLE

Georgian town planning, laid out by John Baxter, who had worked under William Adam. When the Duke of Gordon had the old village demolished a new square was created with fine houses and a beautiful classical church with symmetrical blocks on either side. The Tudor Revival High School (1846) makes a piquant stylistic contrast with it.

In Edingburgh, Robert Reid and William Sibbald (1802-6) planned Heriot Row, Abercromby Place and Great King Street, and then Archibald Elliott extended Princes Street as far as Calton Street, designing Waterloo Place and the fine buildings grouped round Regent's Bridge. From 1822 Gillespie Graham added Randolph Crescent, Ainslie Place and Moray Place, their centres and corner blocks decked with Tuscan pilasters and half columns. The central gardens formed a complement to the artificial formality of the terraces, an effect admired by Palladians and all lovers of the picturesque. The imaginative use of the city's striking topography exemplifies how classic architecture can be successfully disposed within a 'romantic' natural setting, both elements being harmonised into a unified design at once forceful and sophisticated. What has survived from the hundred years following the inception of the New Town in 1760 justifies the claim that Edinburgh is the most complete Romantic Classical city still to be seen.

The more simplified and refined late Georgian terrace is exemplified by the plain facade and clean-cut window openings of Bon-Accord Crescent, Aberdeen, the work of Archibald Simpson, a local architect of distinction, who also did the square of the same name, a number of churches and the Music Hall in Union Street.

9. Engineering and revivialism c 1800 to c 1900

The industrial revolution was well under way by 1760 and the background to the urban prosperity manifest in the new Georgian streets and squares of the larger towns was the rapid expansion of trade and manufacturing which was transforming the nature of British society. The great civil engineers of the period provided the new roads, canals, railway works, bridges, warehouses and docks for the new industrial society.

John Smeaton, who constructed the Forth and Clyde Canal and bridges at Coldstream and Perth, was a Yorkshireman and a contemporary of James Brindley, but most of the other great names of a later generation were Scots.

Remembered chiefly for the immense dock works in London and many other large British ports, including Leith, and for his great bridges over the River Thames in London, John Rennie also built bridges in Scotland. A very fine example is the sturdy but gracefully proportioned bridge of five spans over the river Tweed at Kelso (Borders), which he built about 1800 as a model for the old Waterloo Bridge, demolished in the 1930s. As is usual with bridges at this time, the detail, with its pairs of applied Doric columns to each pier, is classical. Musselburgh (Lothian) has another Rennie bridge, besides its old medieval one.

Thomas Telford, who began as a stone mason, was one of the greatest engineers of his time and his work embraced all forms of civil engineering. McAdam is famous for road construction and new roadmaking techniques but it was Telford who constructed hundreds of miles of difficult mountain roads in Scotland. He was chief engineer of the ambitious Caledonian Canal (1803-47) with its impressive flight of locks near Corpach (Highland); he laid out Pulteneytown, Wick (Highland) and built many bridges, such as Dunkeld (Tayside). Most of his Scottish bridges were of stone but technically more adventurous were his iron bridges. He had an instinctive aesthetic sense like many good engineers and at Craigellachie (Grampian) in 1815 he designed the fine bridge over the Spey, its lattice-work arch abutted by two crenellated towers in the picturesque manner of the period. His masterpiece is Dean Bridge (1831), Edinburgh, 100 foot (30 m) high viaduct which reaches impressively across the Water of Leith. In contrast there is a diminutive but graceful early suspension bridge with turret-gateway pylons at Melrose (Borders) (1820).

The grandfather of Robert Louis Stevenson, Robert Stevenson, was the distinguished builder of twenty-three Scottish lighthouses, of which the greatest is perhaps the Bell Rock

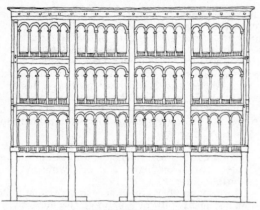

GARDNER'S BUILDING

on Inchcape Rock off Arbroath (Tayside). One son Alan built the elegant Skerryvore lighthouse (1844) near Tiree (Strathclyde) and another son, Thomas, that on Kinnaird's Head, Fraserburgh (Grampian), on top of an old tower.

These men put Scotland in the front rank of technological progress throughout the world. Their work is extremely impressive. For essential simplicity and grandeur of impact it recalls the bridges and aqueducts of ancient Rome, but its scale is often entirely without precedent, as for instance the West Highland Railway viaduct at Glen Finnan (Highland), which passes over the Road to the Isles.

By the early nineteenth century iron was being used structurally in warehouses and commercial buildings and by the mid century cast iron fronts appeared in America. From 1855 dates the Gardner's Building, Glasgow, with its external frame of attenuated Doric columns supporting entablatures, with delicate arcading between, following the trend of designs of the time executed in stone.

The Victorian *tour de force,* the 4¼ mile (6.8 km) mild steel railway bridge over the Forth, was the work of Sir Benjamin Baker and Sir John Fowler, completed in 1889 after seven years. Great approach viaducts lead towards the three magnificently functional cantilever spans with their massive network of girders and struts. It is a design of epic quality and a climax to the effort of the century. Five thousand men were employed on it at one time.

In the early nineteenth century, Greek revival or neo-Greek became, in its various versions, an international style for buildings as diverse and far apart as the British Museum and the

Capitol, Washington DC. The German scholar Winckelmann in particular, whose book was published in 1763, was among the first to show a true appreciation of the essential qualities of Greek as distinct from Roman classicism. But a year earlier — before Robert Adam had made his impact — Stuart and Revett's *Antiquities of Athens* had been published in Britain. Stuart, who had visited Athens in 1751, became known as 'Athenian' Stuart. His garden temple at Hagley Park (Hereford and Worcester) (1758) is the first archaeologically correct use of Greek Doric in Britain and in 1763 he employed Ionic at Lichfield House, St James's Square, London.

The style was later fostered and rapidly spread after the travels in Greece of architects like Cockerell, Smirke and Inwood, and in 1801 the arrival from Athens of the Parthenon sculptures aroused further interest.

In one form or another it became a style peculiarly identified at this time with the spirit of Edinburgh and Glasgow, where it lasted longest and was most consistent. The dignified urbanity which resulted has not been excelled. The notable Scottish exponents were Playfair and Hamilton in Edinburgh, 'Greek' Thompson in Glasgow and Simpson in Aberdeen.

William Henry Playfair was born in London, trained in Glasgow with Starkie, benefited from working with talents as diverse as the erratic James Wyatt and the solid Smirke, and did his best work in Edinburgh. In 1815 he was commissioned to carry out the eastern extension of the earlier plan of the New Town to Calton Hill and his work is exemplified by the Royal Circus and the impressive Calton, Royal and Regent Terraces, the last a grave repetitive quarter-mile (400 m) facade with gardens to the rear laid out by Sir James Paxton. He also did a large number of other works including the Royal Scottish Academy (the old Royal Institution) in massive Doric (1822) and the National Gallery of Scotland (1850) in Ionic, both off Princes Street opposite the cross axis of the New Town. He remodelled and extended the Adams' University building (1816-24) (adding a great quadrangle, a fine neo-Doric portico and the library hall, a fine interior) and designed the Advocates' Library interior (exterior by Archibald Elliott), the College of Surgeons (Ionic), St Stephen's Church (Renaissance with a hint of Gothic) and, on Calton Hill, the Observatory and Doric memorial to his astronomer uncle, and the unfinished Scottish National Monument (with C. R. Cockerell) — to commemorate the dead of the Napoleonic struggle — begun in the manner of the Parthenon. Outside Edinburgh, Playfair designed the highly successful Academy at Dollar (Central), an early work of 1818 from which he gained much experience. Two more classical school buildings of the 1830s are Bathgate Academy (Lothian), with its colonnaded wings, and Banff Academy (Grampian) with its impressive Ionic portico.

Despite Playfair's overwhelming preference for Greek revival, like many British architects of the period he did not consider himself confined to one form of revivalism. He added a gateway and lodge to Heriot's Hospital and built Donaldson's Hospital and the twin-towered New College (1846) — originally of the Free Kirk — Edinburgh, in a neo-Tudor style on the slopes of the Old Town. In England Nash exhibited the same kind of virtuosity and later Sir George Gilbert Scott, when occasion required it. Other examples are David Rhind's Daniel Stewart's College (1849), Fettes College, the Edinburgh Royal Infirmary and the attractive Orphan Hospital by Thomas Hamilton.

One of the finest achievements in neo-Greek, however, is Thomas Hamilton's Royal High School, Edinburgh, 1825. It has a superb site backed by acropolis-like Calton Hill and is an adaptation of the best preserved of the Doric temples, that of Theseus in Athens. It is a complex design. The disposition of its masses is skilful, its detail crisp and precise, but beyond any list of physical qualities is the imaginative way in which romantic overtones are extracted from what might have been a work of cool classical detachment. Facing it is the same architect's Burns Monument, closely based on the temple or choragic monument of Lysicrates in Athens.

Among Hamilton's best buildings is the Royal College of Physicians, Queen Street, a late work of 1854, which without any of the plagiarism of the Burns Monument exhibits essentially Greek feeling expressed in what is really a Graeco-Roman design of considerable originality, grace and charm.

William Burn, mainly a Gothicist, designed the John Watson and Merchant Maiden Hospitals, the fine Doric Custom House, Greenock (Strathclyde), and the Melville column in St Andrew Square, which he modelled on Trajan's column.

The seventeenth-century Parliament House (now Court of Session and High Court), Edinburgh, with its curious fine timber roof that seems a cross between a hammer-beam type and imitation pendant vaulting, was given a facelift by Robert Reid when a pedimented propyleum was added over a rusticated and arcaded ground floor. Nearby is the Signet Library with its splendid Roman Corinthian Upper Hall by William Stark, about 1812, perhaps the most magnificent room in Edinburgh.

Gray's Hospital, Elgin (Grampian), built by the Edinburgh architect James Gillespie Graham, in 1815, has an impressive portico and a central cupola rising from an octagonal base. Also in Elgin Anderson's Institution (1831) is a Greek Revival design dignified with a tall dome and classical porticoes, Doric and Ionic, and the church of St Giles (about 1826) is the work of

Archibald Simpson.

In Glasgow striking works of the period are David Hamilton's Graeco-Roman Royal Exchange (1829), although it falls below the standard set by Thomas Hamilton and Playfair in Edinburgh, and Aitkenhead House (1806), Hutcheson's Hospital and the Nelson monument. The Exchange, now Stirling's Library, began as a private house in 1780, became a bank, and then the Royal Exchange, when an impressive portico was added in 1827.

Later remodelling has retained Stark's Doric facade of the Justiciary Building (1814), Glasgow, and the immensely successful London architect Decimus Burton, another Greek revivalist and author of the London Atheneum, designed Kelvinside estate about 1840 with more imposing neo-Greek terraces.

Alexander Thomson, nicknamed 'Greek' Thomson, though he had never been to Greece, became the outstanding name in Greek revival in Glasgow. He was evidently able to work in a variety of styles for his early houses have a Scottish baronial flavour, but he soon showed his real bent in his designs in the 1850s and 1860s for the monumental Great Western Road terraces and the Free Church and Presbyterian churches of Caledonia Road, Queens Park and St Vincent Street, the last dating from 1857, a strangely splendid composition showing skilful treatment of an awkward sloping site. These late essays in modified neo-Greek were scholarly creative transpositions of the mode to new types of building exhibiting astonishing resourcefulness and sense of style. His chief master appears to have been Schinkel, of Berlin, but there was in Thomson a highly original and imaginative exotic streak that absorbed even Egyptian and Hindu influences and made them a part of his individual eclectic version of the Romantic classical style.

Queens Park (1867) is perhaps his masterpiece, topped with an 'oriental' tower, but the interior too, like that of the galleried Caledonia Road, is distinguished, and particularly interesting is his frank use of elegant iron columns and painted decoration. Caledonia Road has the asymmetrical western tower associated with mid-Victorian Gothic revival and a beautiful hexastyle porch rising from a podium. The success of the more orthodox Greek revival of the elegant Moray Place, Strathbungo, Glasgow, and the later Great Western Terrace, however, had a salutory influence on much Glasgow architecture of the time.

There were interpretations of various other types of classicism right through the century, particularly in Glasgow, where Clarke and Bell did sound work in both Greek and Renaissance, as in the County Buildings (1844) and the Fish Market facade (1873). Charles Wilson's Royal Faculty of Procurators (1854) is a small but choice essay in the style of the Venetian High Renaissance, boldy modelled with a fine staircase in the Genoese manner. The

ROYAL FACULTY OF PROCURATORS

Bank of Scotland, St Vincent Place, is a more grandiose exercise in the Italian High Renaissance style of about 1869.

George Square, Glasgow, had been laid out as a Georgian square a hundred years earlier when William Young, the architect of the War Office in Whitehall, produced his design for the massive Municipal Buildings (1889) on the east side of the square. Now known as the City Chambers, this is a powerful well composed building. The principal front has a pedimented and turreted centre section with three tiers of coupled columns linked by bold horizontal cornices and colonnades to impressive domed corner towers. The main entrance leads into a great loggia modelled on an Italian Renaissance church and decked out in a rich display of materials: stone, granite, marble and mosaic. Imposing staircases lead to the upper floors, where there are a grand banqueting hall, ornate reception saloons, the council chamber and a long vista of round arches and spacious marble halls.

Large handsome Italianate churches were built in Cathedral Square and Westbourne Gardens about 1880 by John Honeyman, who had already built the fine 'Early English' Lansdowne Church — with its exceptionally slender spire — nearly twenty years before.

In Edinburgh, too, the preference for neo-Greek was not exclusive, especially in commercial buildings, which now constituted some of the largest commissions. Antedating any of the big London banks, David Rhind's Commercial Bank of Scotland in George Street (1846) has a monumental portico but has abandoned Grecian detail; Bryce's British Linen Bank in St Andrew Square (1852) is a boldly modelled Italianate design.

Only three years later Rhind's Life Association of Scotland building in Princes Street marks a further step away from the purity of neo-Greek, this time to a rich and vigorous High Renaissance mode, like that of a Venetian palazzo. There are also the massive Venetian Renaissance Royal Scottish Museum, dating from the 1860s, and at the end of the century, St Cuthbert's, Edinburgh, in an early Renaissance manner. Gothic revival was generally the received style of ecclesiastical buildings after about 1830. Better known for his Gothic work, Sir R. Rowland Anderson's design for the Medical College is Italian Renaissance. The two polarities of the century were classicism and revivalism. The Gothic revival took a form as characteristic as neo-Greek had earlier, the medievalism of 'Scottish baronial' more often than not modified by foreign styles, usually French.

Edward Blore and William Atkinson built the somewhat eclectic Abbotsford near Melrose (Borders) in 1816 for Sir Walter Scott. Scott's reputation ensured its success and Abbotsford exerted a powerful influence on the course taken by medieval revivalism in Scotland. It was a manifestation of Scott's national feeling with its strong historical sense and antiquarian enthusiasm, and it is to be viewed against the background of interest in a romanticised medieval period which literature was taking at this time. In 1829 William Burn remodelled a classical house, Tyninghame (Lothian), and produced a romantic Scottish baronial design.

The famous Scott Monument in Princes Street, Edinburgh, a huge Gothic arched baldacchino from which springs a soaring spire, was created by G. Meikle Kemp. Richly florid, this a splendid romantic foil to the cool, massive classicism of Playfair's nearby Academy and National Gallery.

Floors Castle at Kelso (Borders) is an example of W. H. Playfair's Tudor-style work. Well sited by the River Tweed, it was originally designed by William Adam, perhaps from a scheme suggested by Sir John Vanbrugh about 1718. But in 1838 Playfair added the elaborate turrets, cupolas and battlements. This conception of architecture is of something to be assumed by a building, a historical costume that bears little relation to the character of the house and nothing at all to its functional purpose. Playfair did include a ballroom, however. The entrance gates are as recent as 1929.

At Lauriston Castle, Edinburgh, a banker turned a sixteenth-century tower into a rambling medieval house about 1830; but it was Prince Albert who established at Balmoral (Grampian) the fashion for castellated mansions. The first house had been built in the 1830s by John Smith and his son, William, carried out the much vaster reconstruction of Prince Albert's in 1853, in the same style. Typically Albert combined romance and practicality

BALMORAL CASTLE

and had the 'castle' equipped with a prefabricated iron ballroom manufactured in Manchester by Bellhouse, who had produced houses for Australian emigrants on a similar principle and shown them at the Great Exhibition.

Blair Castle (Tayside) is a ducal mansion of an old site, like Inveraray. Its nucleus was Comyn's Tower of 1269 and it was transformed into a large country house in the middle of the eighteenth century. But its present aspect owes much to its castellation in the revived baronial style, which was the work of David Bryce about 1869.

Examples of his commercial work are the pretentious classical Renaissance Bank of Scotland on the Mound, Edinburgh, and the premises of the British Linen Bank in St Andrew Square, and of his institutional buildings the Edinburgh Royal Infirmary. One of his oddest commissions was the mausoleum he built in 1840 at Hamilton (Strathclyde) for the ducal house of that name. It is a massive box, pilastered and arcaded, supporting a drum and a hemispherical dome. The masonry is dovetailed and virtually unmortared and the bronze doors are embellished with scriptural reliefs. It is an extraordinary work of architectural 'sculpture' rather than a building and at the same time a kind of pretentious 'folly' comparable to that other 'Roman' work, the Colosseum-like structure on Oban Hill (Strathclyde), 1900, and the temple mausoleum for a Lancashire manufacturer on the island of Rum but curiously compelling all the same. At Dundee the Victoria Gate (1844) is virtually a 'Norman' folly.

Dunrobin Castle (Highland) dates from 1275, but the main part is mid-Victorian as it was remodelled and extended by Sir Charles Barry, 1835-50. It is an impressive embodiment of great riches and aristocratic hauteur but it lacks the refinement and elegance of the great houses of the eighteenth century.

Inverness Castle is early Victorian Gothic whereas Beaufort Castle, Lord Lovat's seat near Beauly (Highland), is an

117

elaborate work of the 1880s. Carbisdale Castle is another large Victorian baronial mansion in Highland. Ingliston House (Lothian) is neo-Scottish baronial of 1846 but one of the most bizarre examples is Kinettles near Forfar (Tayside).

The baronial style extended to the villas of the prosperous commercial and professional middle classes. In Edinburgh the Victorian villas in Merchiston, Murrayfield, the Grange and Ravelston Dykes are redolent of the period. Among the best are Thomson's very original houses in the Glasgow suburbs of Langside and Cathcart from the 1850s.

James Gillespie Graham's neo-Perpendicular St Andrew's Roman Catholic Cathedral, Glasgow (1816), is interesting as being the first attempt at a genuine Gothic revival in the city but the most prominent Gothicist in Britain during the mid nineteenth century was Sir George Gilbert Scott, whose speciality was a version of revivalism based on the Decorated of the fourteenth century. His new building for Glasgow University that went up in the 1860s has its critics, but the vast range standing on Gilmorehill is a most impressive Victorian monument, its stately 300 foot (90 m) tower a dominant accent in the skyline of modern Glasgow. The style was used first in the Albert Insitute, Dundee.

Shortly afterwards Scott won the competition for St Mary's Episcopalian Cathedral, Edinburgh. A huge church with three tall spires, it was built in the 1870s in the early Gothic revival favoured by the purists, who preferred it to what they regarded as the more materialistic styles of later Gothic. It makes an abrupt contrast with the Georgian terraces which surround it. The western spires were not added until the time of the First World War but the choir school is the old house of Easter Coates and goes back to the seventeenth century.

Revived in the Wallace Memorial (1861) as a national Gothic feature was the crown spire of the later medieval period, widely used in Victorian church architecture. William Young gave one to the parish church at Peebles (Borders) and so did H. P. Blanc, the Edinburgh architect, to his Decorated Coats Memorial Church, Paisley (Strathclyde). There were Gothic town halls too, Inverness (Highland) and Renfrew (Strathclyde) being among them. The parish church at Strathbungo, Glasgow, is a neo-Romanesque design by W. G. Rowan; a better one is his St Ninian's, Cathcart Road (1888).

Another great university building of the period is that of Marischal College, a twin college with King's in the University of Aberdeen. Founded in the late sixteenth century, the present structure is an imposing, profusely pinnacled edifice in white granite, the material so characteristic of the city.

Until the later eighteenth century people did not travel much in Scotland. There were few inns and not many of these were large or well appointed. Most could have been little more than ale houses or hedge inns, like the diminutive thatched Tam O'Shanter, in Ayr (Strathclyde). In the bigger towns on the coaching routes larger establishments grew up in the seventeenth or eighteenth centuries, inns like the Cross Keys, Kelso (Borders), and in Edinburgh, in Canongate, the restored seventeenth-century White Horse Inn (forestairs leading to timbered galleries), which was a well known coaching terminus.

But the nineteenth century and the railways were to change the situation with remarkable speed. When from the middle of the century Thomas Cook began his Scottish tours for the middle class traveller, and Victoria and Albert in buying Balmoral set the fashion for the upper classes, Scotland became the objective of an increasingly large number of tourists. 'Hunting lodges' proliferated, and hotels began to appear in the most favoured areas. Some were quite large and inherited something of the tradition of the country house. Among the largest are the Atholl Palace, Pitlochry (Tayside), and the Glengarry Castle, Invergarry (Highland). Gleneagles (Tayside) is a reminder that the international spread of a national game, golf, helped this movement, as well as the railways, which reached their apotheosis in the great terminus hotels like the North British and Caledonian at each end of Princes Street, Edinburgh.

The dignified *Scotsman* building commanding the North Bridge, Edinburgh, shows how the baronial style could be adapted to commercial and office buildings. On the other hand John Burnet senior's Glasgow Stock Exchange is in 'Franco-Venetian Gothic' and the 'Doge's Palace', a carpet factory adjoining Glasgow Green, is a fantasy of 'Venetian' polychrome brick and tile by William Leiper, who built the old Sun Life office in West George Street in a grand Early French Renaissance style. The County Buildings at Haddington (Lothian) are an essay in 'Jacobean' by William Burn.

As the century wore on, the variety of revival styles multiplied and buildings can no longer be classified with any accuracy under neat stylistic labels though they generally continue to march vaguely under either the 'Renaissance' or the 'Gothic' banner. Many Victorian Gothicists tended to misunderstand the essential nature of the genuine article and misapplied its characteristic features in a rather insensitive way.

Sir Robert Rowand Anderson, however, was one of the most accomplished Scottish architects working at the end of the nineteenth century; his work embraced a number of important buildings in a variety of styles. Besides Mount Stuart (Bute, Strathclyde), the National Portrait Gallery and the National Museum of Antiquities (1890) in Decorated Gothic, with parts representative of other periods, it includes the Medical College in Italian Renaissance and the McEwan Hall with its Grecian theatre interior. In Glasgow the Central Station Hotel is characteristically monumental.

These are examples of the kind of academic work which could be expected from the most able men of the profession at this time. But Rowand Anderson is also remembered for the salutary influence he exerted in promoting a proper understanding of the native tradition of building that implied more than just a superficial, imitative revivalism. His collection of measured drawings became the nucleus of the National Art Survey Drawings, intended to 'serve the purpose of recording and developing Scottish tradition in building'. It was in this spirit that he carried out the restoration of Dunblane Cathedral (Central), where Sir Robert Lorimer was also engaged.

The chancel of St Bride's, Glasgow, is by G. F. Bodley, one of the later medievalists who kept closer to original Gothic than most Victorians, and his churches have a real sensitivity and devotional feeling about them. Most of his work was curvilinear Middle Pointed or Decorated.

Perhaps most widely known for the elaborate chapel of the Knights of the Thistle in St Giles' Cathedral and the National War Memorial in Edinburgh Castle, Lorimer was articled to Sir R. Rowand Anderson and then employed by Bodley. In addition to the restoration at Dunblane Cathedral, Lorimer's church work includes restorations to Paisley Abbey (Strathclyde) and St John's, Perth, where in the north transept he designed a war memorial chapel. At St Peter's, Falcon Avenue, Edinburgh, he designed a church that gives a remarkable experience of spaciousness for a relatively small interior, and a late work, St Margaret's, Glasgow (1925), in a simple Scandinavian manner has exceptional interior woodwork.

The Aberdonian Sir John Ninian Comper was born in the same year as Lorimer and articled to the firm of Bodley and Garner. Gaining a reputation for sumptuous church decoration, in particular stained glass, he was also responsible for complete church designs, of which a good specimen is Kirriemuir (Tayside), which preserves in its fabric the gable of the old kirk.

Among the very few Victorians who deviated from the movement was Philip Webb, who built the famous Red House for his friend William Morris and did much to sponsor good design but unfortunately his output was very limited. Scotland, however, has a rare example in the country house he built at Arisaig (Highland) in 1863. This was his first large country house and while its elevations of local stone are rather conventional High Victorian Gothic its internal arrangement with principal rooms round a two-storeyed central hall is a notable one.

10. The twentieth century

Gothic revival continued into the first part of the twentieth century, one of the best examples being the cathedral church at Troon (Strathclyde), 1910, a monumental design of much interest by Reginald Farlie, a pupil of Sir Robert Lorimer. Among the Scottish pioneers of a modern style was Charles Rennie Mackintosh, whose work is a link between the Arts and Crafts movement inspired by William Morris and the internationalism of the modernist.

Articled to and later a partner in the firm of Honeyman and Keppie Glasgow, to whose *Glasgow Herald* building he contributed, Mackintosh won the competition for the School of Art in 1896, a building which brought him international fame. The bold straightforward lines of the earliest part are marked by a deliberate asymmetery and a horizontality that contrasts with the later vertical north end with its fewer and varied window shapes. The elongated oriels are particularly dramatic and effective. Within, besides its originality of decoration, the library has that recognisably modern handling of space which defines without enclosing. It is a composition in which Mackintosh blends boldness and subtlety with a consummate architectural sense.

In planning, structural design, use of materials, spatial values and interior decoration the Art School manifests a refreshing break with all that had gone before and in this way helped the struggling modern movement to attain a new honesty and integrity unencumbered by the imitation of the past.

Although Mackintosh shared the practical, functional spirit of Scottish vernacular architecture of the seventeenth century, there is no question of a 'period' style and nowhere is this more apparent than in the decorative wiry ironwork of the railings and windows (the 'grilles' are perhaps an echo of the later tower houses) where the famous 'art nouveau' motifs are displayed.

The non-functional art nouveau element in Mackintosh's work linked up with those trends in Belgium and France in the 1890s which were part of a totally new system of design based on rather attenuated lines and flowing forms. The version of Mackintosh and his wife, however, was distinctive — the stickwork for example — as may be seen from the library at the Art School and in their designs for the decoration of Cranston's tearooms in Glasgow, notably the Willow Tea Room in Sauchiehall Street.

When he visited the Vienna Exhibition of 1900 Mackintosh was fêted as a British master of the new style and it was in Austria and Holland in the early twentieth century, the crucial years when the foundations of modern architecture were being laid in Europe, that his influence was most strongly felt.

But unfortunately, lacking recognition at home, he gave up practice prematurely in 1913 and so has left us little work to enjoy. There is the Scotland Street School of 1904, its straight-forward front pierced by horizontal window openings with strong stone grids, and with flanking stair towers, and there are examples of his domestic work showing something of his freshness of approach and new simplicity: Windy Hill, Kilmacolm (Strathclyde) and Hill House and Blackie House, Helensburgh (Strathclyde). The gable, chimney stacks and turret of the last are more than usually obvious echoes of the picturesque Scottish castle, but something too is perhaps owed to C. F. A. Voysey. The abstract geometrical elements and the original interiors are, however, Mackintosh's own. Hous'Hill, Nitshill, Glasgow, has a music room that shows his remarkable spatial sense. His Queen's Cross Church, Maryhill, Glasgow, too has art nouveau touches, and the hall in Ruchill Street is also by his hand.

Gullane (Lothian), a golfing resort within reach of the capital, shows how the Edwardians carried on the upper-middle class villa tradition of the Victorian age with modifications owing something to the Arts and Crafts movement and the work of C. R. Mackintosh and C. F. A. Voysey, who brought a new simplicity into domestic architecture. An impressive example is Greywalls (now a hotel) by Sir Edwin Lutyens.

Sir John Burnet, who trained at the Beaux Arts, Paris, under Pascal, did much work in Scotland, from railway stations to churches. His main public buildings include the 'Austrian Baroque' Elder Library and the extensions to the University and the Western Infirmary, Glasgow. He also did the impressive block, 200 St Vincent Street, Glasgow (1929), and Forsyth's shop in Princes Street, Edinburgh.

The most important commission for a public building in Scotland during the 1930s was that for the new government offices in Edinburgh, St Andrew's House below Calton Hill. By Thomas J. Tait, its superficial modernism exemplifies the use of a very free sort of monumental classic style, without the customary trimmings, at that time deemed suitable for large civic and commercial buildings. Such works represent the last attempts to deck out the twentieth-century steel or concrete-frame building as though it were still constructed of load-bearing walls.

Sir Patrick Geddes of Edinburgh, who coined the word 'conurbation', was one of the great pioneers of modern town planning. A disciple of Geddes, Sir Patrick Abercrombie, with J. H. Forshaw, produced the County of London and Greater London plans on a scale of unprecedented thoroughness. Eventually Abercrombie prepared plans for Edinburgh and the

Clyde Valley (1946) and became recognised internationally as one of the world's outstanding authorities on civic design and town planning. The growth of urban areas has led to a decentralisation from Glasgow. This has created the new towns of East Kilbride and Cumbernauld. Cumbernauld, sited on a long ridge, was designed as a complete urban community with its own industries rather than a dormitory town.

After training in Edinburgh, Sir Basil Spence worked in the office of the great Edwardian Lutyens before going into practice on his own account. Scotland gave him one of his earlier opportunities when he designed the Pavilion for the Empire Exhibition, just before the Second World War. His post-war buildings demonstrate his different and individual solutions to particular architectural problems producing buildings of great character. They include the chapel and library for the University of Edinburgh, the nuclear physics building for Glasgow University, the secondary school at the new town of East Kilbride (Strathclyde), a house at Longniddry (Lothian), and the fishing village at Dunbar (Lothian), where new dwellings harmonise admirably with the narrow streets of red sandstone cottages that wind down to the harbour and yet are entirely contemporary. Further redevelopment shows how good architecture tends to stimulate more of the same kind.

Thurso (Highland) has an eighteenth-century port but the sixteenth-century fishing town is the ancient nucleus. This has been renovated by Sir Frank Mears and new houses built on a plan that is admirably integrated with the old.

In the Canongate scheme, Edinburgh, old fronts like those of Huntly House and Gladstone's Land have inspired new buildings that express traditional ideas in the modern idiom in a thoughtful and sensitive way.

Not until after the Second World War is there any genuinely contemporary architecture in the generally accepted meaning of the term — architecture which wholeheartedly accepts the principles, possibilities and materials of the new international style based upon industrial production. A few representative examples will be considered.

In the new town of Glenrothes (Fife), on the coalfield, Egon Riss's colliery buildings (1955) in concrete, engineering brick and glass are in the best tradition of modern industrial architecture planned and designed on the basis of a careful study of function in detail. The 200 foot (60 m) winding towers of reinforced concrete with metal frame windows and louvres and the shaft hall which links them are new and appropriate architectural expressions of modern winding techniques. The parish kirk by Anthony Wheeler, St Columba's, is a splendid piece of modern ecclesiastical architecture which makes candid

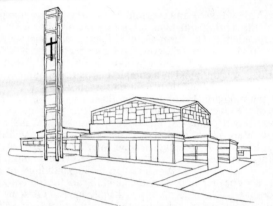

ST COLUMBA'S CHURCH

use of its materials of brick, steel and wood. Its centralised plan is a version of the Greek cross and it too is functionally designed in relation to the post-Reformation service of the Church of Scotland. There is a detached campanile.

Another notable modern church is St Bride's, East Kilbride (Strathclyde) by Gillespie, Kidd and Coia. Also by the same firm is St Mary of the Angels, Camelon (Central) a complicated little building with interesting use of timber construction.

Domestic architecture may be represented by 'High Sunderland', Galashiels (Borders), by Peter Womersley. Completed in 1957, this is a single-storey house constructed chiefly of timber. It has a spreading plan that exemplifies a modern preference for open-planning and the interpenetration of house and garden through the media of terraces and courtyards, which are enclosed by the total structure. More recent is his house at Port Murray, Turnberry (Strathclyde).

At Elgin (Grampian) the new town hall is an example of the contemporary style applied to a civic building and the range to which modern building is now applied can be demonstrated by two examples from Edinburgh: the fine, original Herbarium at the Royal Botanic Garden and the Children's Pavilion at the Astley Ainslie Hospital.

The hydro-electric power station at Glen Lochay near Killin (Central) by Sir Robert H. Matthew is an example of what can be done when an industrial building is erected in an area of high scenic qualities. Rubble walling, roof of copper sheeting that weather agreeably and spruce-wood linings are sympathetically used materials. Although modern in style, the buildings have links with tradition, are well sited, unobtrusive and in admirable harmony with their rural environment.

The Arts and Social Sciences Building for Edinburgh University in George Square (Sir Robert Matthew, Johnson-Marshall, and Partners) is an interesting example of architecture based on a 'module', a fundamental unit, here 4 inches (102 mm), upon which the dimensions of all elements and components are based. Not only does this achieve a mathematical harmony in the design of the building — an ancient classical idea — but it also has far-reaching practical effects in co-ordinating the work of architect, manufacturer and contractor by standardising and thus speeding up work and reducing costs.

University buildings include those of the University of Strathclyde, the Science Library of the University of Aberdeen, the Physics Department at St Andrews (Fife) and at Edinburgh the Departments of Botany and Civil Engineering in Mayfield Road and the David Hume Tower in George Square. The University of Strathclyde stands on a 27 acre (11 ha) site with a large frontage on George Street not far from City Chambers at the centre of Glasgow, and its Social Studies Building is expressive of its transformed character. Technical college buildings of note include the College of Commerce, Glasgow, and the Scottish Woollen Technical College, Selkirk (Borders). Among Glasgow Schools, Hutcheson's Boys Grammar School and schools at King's Park and Barlanark are representative of the best.

Outstanding among recent work, the new home of the Burrell Collection at Pollok, Glasgow, is a rare blend of mastery of technology with humane feeling in a design which shows great verve and self confidence.

The problems of high building and redevelopment in old-established cities remain to be solved. The towers and slabs of the 1950s have been criticised for social reasons. Glasgow has been described, in its architectural aspect, as the most Victorian of British cities and since the revaluation of nineteenth-century architecture this has become a title to be reckoned with. It will be a pity if, in the zest for replanning, much of its irreplaceable character is to be swept away.

Bibliography

Cruden, S. H. *The Scottish Castle*. Nelson, 1960.

Cruden, S. H. *Scottish Abbeys*. HMSO, 1960.

Dickinson, W. C. *Scotland from Earliest Times to 1603*. Nelson 1961.

Feachem, R. *A Guide to Prehistoric Scotland*. Batsford, 1963.

Fletcher, B. *History of Architecture*. Revised by R. A. Cordingley. Athlone Press, 1961.

Gifford, J., *Edinburgh:* the Buildings of Scotland. Penguin, 1985.

MacGibbon, D. and Ross, T., *The Castellated and Domestic Architecture of Scotland*. Edinburgh, 1971.

Pryde, G. S. *Scotland from 1603 to Present Day*. Nelson, 1962.

Salter, Mike. *Discovering Scottish Castles*. Shire Publications, 1985.

Scott-Moncrieff, G. *Edinburgh*. Oliver and Boyd, 1965.

Simpson, W. Douglas. *Illustrated Guide to Ancient Monuments, Volume VI, Scotland*. (Roman, Celtic, Medieval periods.) HMSO, 1961.

Simpson, W. Douglas, *The Ancient Stones of Scotland*. Hale, 1965.

Sinclair, F. *150 Years of Scottish Architecture*. Scottish Academic Press, 1985.

Tranter, N. *The Fortified House in Scotland*. Chambers, 1970.

Young, A. M., and Doak, A. M. *Glasgow at a Glance: an architectural handbook*. Collins, 1965.

Index

INDEX